MAMA RISING

DISCOVERING THE NEW YOU THROUGH MOTHERHOOD

AMY TAYLOR-KABBAZ

HAY HOUSE

Carlsbad, California • New York City
London • Sydney • New Delhi

For Andrina

Published in Australia by: Hay House Australia Pty. Ltd.: www.hayhouse.com.au
Published in the United States by: Hay House, Inc.: www.hayhouse.com
Published in the United Kingdom by: Hay House UK, Ltd.: www.hayhouse.co.uk
Published in India by: Hay House Publishers India: www.hayhouse.co.in

Cover Design by Marque Kabbaz
Typeset by Bookhouse, Sydney
Edited by Margie Tubbs
Author photo by Lauren Abi-Hanna

ISBN: 978-1-4019-6108-4
E-Book ISBN: 978-1-4019-5914-2

10 9 8 7 6 5 4 3 2 1
1st Australian edition, 2019
1st United States edition, 2020

Printed in the United States of America

CONTENTS

Introduction   vii

CHAPTER 1   The Birth of the Mother   1

CHAPTER 2   The Unravelling   14

CHAPTER 3   Towards an Answer   26

CHAPTER 4   Focus One > Kindness   36

CHAPTER 5   Focus Two > Strength   58

CHAPTER 6   Focus Three > Value   78

CHAPTER 7   Focus Four > Grace   96

CHAPTER 8   Focus Five > Trust   111

CHAPTER 9   Focus Six > Connection   124

CHAPTER 10   The Birth of You   148

INTRODUCTION

*Spiritual growth is like childbirth. You dilate, then
you contract. You dilate, then you contract again.
As painful as it all feels, it's the necessary rhythm
for reaching the ultimate goal of total openness.*

— MARIANNE WILLIAMSON

I thought I could compartmentalise my life.

I could be the go-getting, ambitious, fun and free Amy, able to chase the dreams I'd set as a serious teenager hoping to change the world with her work, **and** be the mother I wanted to be. I would lie on the couch, watching my belly move as my first daughter kicked and rolled inside me, and tell myself I could do it all. I could be the best mother and still be me. I wouldn't lose myself. I **could** do it all. After all, that's what our generation was promised we could do.

And then, a few months later, I looked at her. When it was time for my divine, feisty, vulnerable first child to come into this world, I gazed into two of the most pleading eyes I have ever seen, and something changed. While covered in vernix and blood, hastily wrapped in a cloth to keep warm, it was as if she was saying: *Help me, mama.*

She'd only been in the world for a matter of minutes. She'd needed a little help to get started when she first emerged from me, blue after being sucked out with the ventouse at the last minute, after hours of endless labour, airwaves cleared until—finally—that first cry pierced the labour room and I knew she was alright.

But then, straight onto my chest, skin on skin, big blue pleading eyes looking straight into mine: *Please. Help me. I need you.*

And that was it. In that moment, I split into two: the woman I used to be, and her mother.

And for the past eleven years, since that very first moment, I have been trying to figure out what that looks like. How can I possibly not lose myself completely in her needs—and then those of her sister and brother—without giving up on myself? How can I hold her hand and heart and soul through this overwhelming and tough world, and still hold my own too? How can I honour my deep passion for journalism, for storytelling, for changing the world for women, and still ensure I am there for every one of **her** steps, so she can grow up and change the world in her own way.

I didn't know. I honestly didn't know. And for many years, I didn't understand why I found it all so very, very hard.

Those little pleading blue eyes changed into strong, fierce green ones, similar to the flashing green eyes of the woman she was named after—Scarlett O'Hara from *Gone with the Wind*. But her need for me did not. Still hasn't. This child—this gift—has continuously stretched and challenged me in ways I never thought possible. She has demanded more from me than I thought I had. Or thought I could give. And through it all, the same questions have consumed me, over and over again:

> How can I do this?

> How can I be there for her, and still be me?

> How can I be there for her sister and brother, without being completely swallowed up?

> How can I do this without getting to the end of the day, burnt out and yelling from sheer exhaustion?

> How can I do this properly, but not give up on all I had planned for myself too?

We think we can compartmentalise our lives: be who we used to be at work, but a mother at home. Be able to switch between work and play, and then turn on the passion at night. We see ourselves as robotic, our list of to-dos so long and loud that we walk around half-conscious; never really present, always two steps ahead in our mind or hung up on what happened yesterday.

This is what society expects of us—we are expected to raise our families and still be all that we were before as well. It's as if we are being asked to just add 'mother' onto our résumé, but not adjust anything else on that list. In fact, we're not allowed to. We have to be the wife, the worker, the sister, the daughter, the friend we've always been. In the workplace, we're expected to return after a brief maternity leave and sit back in the same chair as the same person, continuing as if nothing has happened. Except that we've added 'perfect mother' to our list too.

So I did. Like millions around the world, I just added it onto my list, and assumed things would get better. Some day. I turned into superwoman to keep up. I pushed my own needs to the bottom of the pile.

But the endless questions continued to haunt me:

> Was it okay that I didn't love it all?
> Was I a good mum if I still loved my career?
> Am I successful if I stop loving my career and choose something else?
> What happened to the equal partnership in my marriage?
> Why does it all have to be up to me?
> And after a while, an even scarier one emerged: Who am I now anyway?
> Because the hardest part of this decade-long journey through motherhood has actually been this: I lost my identity.
> So, who am I now?
> Do I still want the same dreams I set all those years ago?

> Does being the best mother to Scarlett and her two siblings mean I have to give up on those dreams?
> If not, then how the hell do I do this?

The truth is that deep down I didn't know. I didn't know who I was, or what I wanted, or how I was going to make it all work.

I just blindly pushed myself to keep going. But with every fibre of my being, I knew that I'd changed.

Then one day, driving around for the millionth drop-off or pick-up or errand as a mama of three, I happened upon a podcast that changed everything. One single word brought on such an immediate reaction, I had to pull over to sob:

Matrescence. Just as adolescence describes the natural but all-encompassing transition from child to adult, and affects every part of your life, matrescence describes the natural but all-encompassing transition from woman to mother. And it affects every part of your life.

I cried the deep soulful sobs of a woman finally acknowledged.

I cried for all the years I had judged myself for not knowing who I was anymore, and for doubting my inner voice.

I cried for all the times I'd pushed my feelings down, pushed on, burnt myself out, and made myself sick—all in the pursuit of being the woman I used to be.

And I cried for the hundreds and hundreds of mamas who had reached out to me through my blog, my podcast, my first book and my social media, sharing their own pain and deep self-doubt.

Finally, finally, there was a reason for what I had been feeling. And there was an explanation for what I had been trying to explain for a decade.

Motherhood changes you. Every fibre, every cell, every area.

And with a little understanding, support and deep compassion, it will be the making of you.

Matrescence, like adolescence, is the emergence of a whole new identity: physical, emotional, societal, spiritual. It starts with that first thought of pregnancy, and does not really ever end. But until now, we have ignored the massive shifts within a woman (especially beyond the first year), and have assumed she'll go back to who she used to be, just with 'mother' added to the list of what she does.

Matrescence is the emergence of a new identity—mother—while you're still trying to comprehend what happened to the old identity. And it's the acknowledgement of the birth of a whole new you, in every possible way.

Let me be clear. This book is not about the act of mothering. It is not about sleeping, discipline, routines, attachment versus helicopter versus abandonment.

I am not concerned about how you became a mama. I am not concerned about whether your baby was conceived on your honeymoon, on the couch or in a test tube. I am not concerned about whether you gave birth on the bathroom floor, in a birthing suite or in an operating theatre. And I am not concerned about whether you have one baby, three or six.

I am concerned about you—the woman. I am here to speak to the woman who has entered the world of parenthood and is searching for a way to balance who she used to be with who she is now.

Because we need a new way. We need to change the way we view motherhood, if we are to stop this endless cycle of burnout and overwhelm. We have to ask new questions and find new answers. We can't just keep allowing women to break down, fall apart and question it all as they experience birth, breastfeeding, broken sleep, relationship difficulties and deep inner searching on their own. We can't just tell them, 'That's just motherhood. It will pass.'

Over the coming pages, I hope that you find the same huge exhale I felt, when I first began to understand that 'it's not just me'.

I have spent the last ten years speaking to thousands of women around the world about their experience of becoming and being a mother, and have dedicated myself to tracking down and interviewing the very best experts in the world on what happens to a woman in these years of matrescence, and how we can best move through it with ease and grace. In the coming chapters, you will find all of this insight—all the voices, the stories, the research and the facts—bundled together to support you as you move through your own season of 'becoming'—no matter how old your kids are.

I hope that the combination of my story, the very latest info from around the world, plus interviews with experts, gives you permission to start looking at this time in your life differently.

There's a reason you feel the way you do, mama, and every single mother out there, rich or poor, black or white, gay or straight, is going through the same thing: the emergence of a new you.

That's the most reassuring thing about understanding matrescence: like adolescence, it is unavoidable. But with the help of the stories I share with you, I hope you'll begin to realise that **this is the birth of a divine new you**.

Dr Catherine Birndorf is the Co-Founder and Medical Director of The Motherhood Center of New York City. I flew to New York and toured the Centre in late 2018, and was deeply affected by the loving, supportive space Dr Birndorf, her co-founder and team had created. This is what all mothers should have. This was the circle of elders, the secret women's business, the space where we all needed to hear those whispers about the wisdom of matrescence. In Dr Birndorf's words:

> When we look at motherhood and matrescence, it really is all about identity. You are never the same—your identity has changed forever. People think 'once I get pregnant, then it will be okay'. Or 'once I have the baby, I won't be so anxious'.

You always think that at some point in the future, things will change. Well, can I say that as a mama with a 16-year-old and a 19-year-old, I believe I am still in matrescence. I am still struggling at times to understand what it means! I can't say I have mastered all of it, but in terms of my own identity, it has been a chronic morphing of myself. It is a complete redefining. And you must have a real sense of self to move through this.

This is where we find our sense of self.

Motherhood is a spiritual awakening, mama. As long as we see it this way, and have the tools and framework around us, it can be the birth of you. And it is magnificent.

So … welcome to the new you!

CHAPTER 1

THE BIRTH OF THE MOTHER

> The critical transition period which has been missed
> is matrescence: the time of mother-becoming ...
> Giving birth does not automatically make a mother
> out of a woman ... The amount of time it takes to
> become a mother needs study.
>
> — DANA RAPHAEL

There is a generation of women who feel as if they are coming last in every aspect of their lives.

Their days are filled with the heaviness of looking after everyone else. The concept of self-care or 'me time' feels like a cruel luxury that only celebrities and Instagram It Girls get to have. Massages. Perfect green smoothies. Nannies looking after the kids so they can build their million-dollar businesses. They flick through the images on their phones while their kids run wild around the playgrounds, and feel even more frumpy and forgotten.

And so they give up.

They get to the end of the day, exhausted and aching. They turn the TV on, numbing the pain with mindless entertainment. Or chocolate. Or wine. They know they should sleep—it's what they ache for all day. But if they don't use those night-time hours to do something even a little 'adult-like', they'll go mad.

They don't know why they feel this way. Isn't this what they wanted? What they've chosen? Whether the baby was unplanned or not, at some point along the way they've opted into this life of 'mother'. So why does it feel so hard?

They want to be calmer, more present. They want to notice the little moments with their children, but they have to do **all the things**. And any talk otherwise just breeds resentment: 'Sure, I'd love to just drop it all and make homemade playdough with my child! But who else is going to clean the house, do the washing, cook the dinner, and RSVP to the two birthday parties this weekend?'

I know. I've been there. And I've listened and nodded as thousands of mamas have sobbed and shared these moments with me too:

> *What's the point? It's too big. I don't have the time, the energy, the money, the support. I collapse at the end of the day and I'm awake all night.*
>
> *I'm just surviving. I can't possibly add anything more to my list.*

I don't know who I am anymore.
I don't recognise myself.
I'm not the person I want to be.

Until something breaks. It's usually the body that goes—we seem to be able to run on broken minds much longer than broken bodies.

It's the cold that never ends, exhaustion, adrenal fatigue. For me, it was my thyroid. And then when that didn't stop me, it was pre-term labour with my son, which finally screamed so loudly that I started to listen.

Only when the body breaks do we start to take notice. Only then do we go to bed early. We get help.

But while we know we need to fix the body, to rebuild it after everything we have put it through, we once again fail to focus on the rest of us. We ignore our feelings, our unhappiness, our overwhelm, our anxiety.

We fail to see the importance of our inner health.

We miss the fact that we are a whole woman, with very real needs, identities and desires. And in the middle of all that we are doing for everyone else, we have big questions:

What happened to me?

Why does it feel like this?

Why can't I seem to get it together and be the mama I want to be?

It's not your fault. It's ours. Society, the community we live in, has failed us. Failed to tell us that what we are feeling is real and legitimate. Failed to acknowledge our pain, our tears and the anxiety that keeps us awake at 3am, wondering how we're ever going to manage it all. And failed to tell us that what we're feeling is real.

For success-driven, modern women, pregnancy is often the very first time we've had to accept that we are not totally in control of our own lives.

We're the generation of women who were given career-advice classes, not classes in home economics and mothering skills. Our ten-year plans were more likely to include buying a home, becoming a CEO and travelling through Europe, than popping a baby out. But like millions of women of our generation, we soon realised that those ten-year plans lacked something. Contentment. Love. True passion. And so we opened our lives up to babies.

But then, motherhood is nothing like we expected. Despite all the preparation, the antenatal classes, and the millions of books we can now download and study, it's a shock. It brings us to our knees. For some, it's instant. For others, it's not until the second baby arrives, or they go back to work, or someone gets sick. But whenever it happens, it will happen. And that's because it's meant to.

I truly believe that becoming a mother is a rite of passage, and a soul awakening. It's part of the cycle of being a woman, of 'becoming'. Because, at the very centre of our souls, and in every cell of our body, we change. We transform. We are different.

Physically, mentally, spiritually. We change on a cellular level and on a soul level.

I know you know this, because you can feel it. The things you used to be passionate about have changed, and the things you never even noticed before have suddenly become really important. You worry about the world your child will grow up in, and you don't care as much whether your neighbour thinks you're nice or not.

Life gets put into perspective.

But it's also confusing as hell. Where has that go-getting career woman gone? What happened to that clear path you had planned out? And what about your relationships, your body, your place in the world? Nothing is the same and that's a scary thing to navigate, while you're also trying to figure out how the hell to get through each day.

There's a reason you feel this way. A very good reason. It's called **matrescence**. Although you may not have heard of that word until now, I promise you that it's the key to the greatest self-compassion and self-awareness. It's the answer to all you've been feeling. It's the language you've been grasping for, when trying to explain to everyone around you why you've been acting the way you have. It's the framework that the world needs to start to use, to begin valuing and supporting mothers more.

How I wish I'd known what matrescence was before I became a mother! My heart aches with the knowing of how different it would have been. How much kinder I would have been on myself.

How much more I could have enjoyed those really traumatic early days, months and years.

Back in 2007, after the birth of my first daughter, Scarlett, I stood at the window of the maternity ward believing that I was the most powerful woman on earth. Despite it being a far-from-perfect birth, all I could think about was how amazing it was that I'd created and birthed a new life. Part oxytocin, part newborn baby awe, I felt invincible.

It's no coincidence that we called my daughter Scarlett. My favourite movie of all time is *Gone with the Wind*; growing up, Scarlett O'Hara was my ultimate hero. Strong, independent and feisty as hell, she was what I longed to be. A day after giving birth, as I stood overlooking the Adelaide parklands in the middle of a scorching heatwave, I felt like my hero. I silently repeated to myself, 'As God is my witness, I will never doubt myself again.' And I believed it.

Sure, the birth was a bit of a horror. I was totally unprepared for the realities of a posterior baby and days of pre-labour stop/start contractions. When the real waves of contractions kicked in just minutes after being induced, I was terrified. My mantras were *I'm never doing this again* and *I can't do this*, repeated over and over again in my head. All I remember is feeling so very, very alone. Terrified of each coming contraction, and alone.

Despite completing the Calmbirth course at my local yoga studio, there was nothing calm about it. It was a terrifying and traumatic experience—and the fear that filled every muscle in my body only made the contractions longer and more excruciating.

Hours later and with no feeling from my waist down, I finally pushed my beautiful baby out, in the most undignified moment of my life. Legs in stirrups, a room full of strangers, and a suction cap stuck to my baby's head. But once she emerged, had been checked by the paediatrician and placed on my chest, I didn't care. Those blue, blue eyes staring up at me changed me in an instant, and the birth of me began.

It wasn't until weeks later, when I found myself retelling the birth story over and over again, that I started to feel less empowered by the inclusion of 'epidural', 'ventouse' and 'stitches'. The oxytocin that surges through our bodies after birth had kept the reality of what I'd just been through at bay long enough for me to have my Scarlett O'Hara moment at the window. So I glowed, like so many new mamas, for the first hours of my daughter's life.

But then, Scarlett wouldn't feed. She was born with congenital torticollis (a condition where her neck muscles and one side of her jaw didn't develop properly, because she was too squished inside me), so turning her head to one side was excruciatingly painful. 'Severe breast rejection' is what the nurses called it. Nice. You can imagine what that did to my new mama glow.

I was a mess. I couldn't breastfeed, and my baby was 'broken'. She needed a tiny cast on her foot as that hadn't developed properly and was pushed up against her shin, and she needed daily physio for her neck.

Over the coming months, I bounced from one 'expert' to the next, putting all my faith in everyone else's expertise. I never stopped to listen to my own instincts, because I didn't think I had any. I was scared, confused and thought I was doing it all wrong. I checked myself in as a day patient at the hospital every day for weeks, walking from my home to the ward in a haze, longing to just get there so I could get some help. While I was there, I felt safe—the midwives could settle my baby, and I could learn how to be a mother. But once I was home again, I was lost.

Every day was a struggle with my internal voice, reminding me over and over again that I was a failure. I cried and cried, and I lashed out at my husband for his inability to do anything right. I was also full of the most unfamiliar emotion of all: resentment. I resented the fact that he had gone back to his normal life with his normal job, leaving me every day to figure things out on my own. There were times when I contemplated leaving him, to go and raise my baby with my sister. Surely that would be better? Of course, I adored my little girl, but I hated myself.

And I often wondered whether I'd done the 'right thing' by having a baby. Perhaps my life would have been better without children?

With daily physiotherapy and the guidance of the most amazing lactation consultant, Scarlett grew strong. She could eventually turn her head to feed, and our life started to settle down. But deep in my very core, I had changed forever.

I had completely lost confidence in myself. There was so much shame that I wasn't the mother I thought I should be, and so much grief for the life I used to have—and for the woman I used to be.

Why couldn't I do better? Why didn't I love it like everyone else? And what if I never felt like myself again?

As a successful, headstrong woman, there wasn't anything that I hadn't been able to do before. I had gone to Japan as a naive fifteen-year-old exchange student—totally Japanese-illiterate— and survived. I then decided I wanted to attend university in Tokyo for a year, so I applied for my university's exchange program and made it happen. I wanted to be a journalist for the ABC, so I was. There was nothing I couldn't do, or so I thought.

But that's the thing about motherhood—it's not about control. In fact, it's often our very first experience in life which has absolutely nothing to do with our willpower or idea of success. It is completely and totally out of our hands, and that terrifies us.

Not that we admit that. Oh no, we don't talk about the pain of those early days, weeks and months of motherhood. We hide behind the mask of motherhood, only ever showing the world the Instagram-worthy photos, brushing off the exhaustion and fear in the hope that no-one will judge us. We avoid the in-depth discussions of childbirth that so many of us need in order to heal; and we aren't honest about the sheer difficulty of early breastfeeding. If and when a courageous mother does share her story publicly, we all cheer; finally, someone is telling the truth!

And yet, we stay silent. We're never told that every woman in the world questions herself and her abilities; we suffer in silence, as we pour layer upon layer of guilt onto our exhausted shoulders.

Surely if we just tried harder, did more, gave more, was more, then we'd be perfect, like everyone else?

But sharing our pain is not weak. It is not weak when we begin to truly understand and accept the reason behind the pain: we are changing. Our lives have forever altered, and there is a grieving process connected to that, plus a reconfiguring of everything we knew. There can be no growth without pain, as harsh as that sounds. When something changes form, there is a shedding of the old. That's physics. That's reality. And that's matrescence.

One day when Scarlett was still only a few weeks old, I remember feeling so scared that I was screwing it all up that I called one of my closest soul sisters from those early days of first-time mamahood. Eliza was a few years ahead of me in parenting experience, and is one of the most honest, open and tell-it-like-it-is women you will ever met. Her heart is big, and her ability to say exactly the right thing at the right time (usually with wit that astounds you) is even bigger. So, with my chest tight and the anxiety of my new world closing in on me, I called her.

The words she shared with me that day changed me forever: 'Motherhood is not love at first sight, Amy. Sure, it's lust at first sight, and you know you've found the one, but you still have to fall in love.'

That was the first time someone had acknowledged what I was feeling. I wasn't in love yet. Certainly not with this whole role of 'mother'. Truth be told, I still have days of considering a divorce from it all.

Becoming a mother is not an overnight sensation. It is a process. In fact, even describing it as a process implies there is an end point, but with matrescence there isn't. This journey, this path of becoming that you are on, has no destination. Other than the next stage. That's what is so damn confronting about it.

In those early days, we hang on through the middle of the night and the endless exhaustion because we believe there will be a time when it will end. Which, of course, it does. But then, it seems to be replaced by the next thing. As a mama to a pre-teen, I promise you it doesn't stop. So any attempt to just 'hang on' while it passes might be good in the moment, but continually leaves us holding on in the hope of a solution that never comes.

Let me be clear here. I'm not saying this will never stop being hard. Not at all. However, through an understanding of the deep transformation of motherhood, you will get to a place (much sooner than you think) where you are happier, more connected, more whole than you've ever been. You will look upon yourself and marvel.

But if you keep holding out for that feeling, believing that it's always just around the next corner, birthday or milestone, you'll be split forever.

Your feelings are calling you, mama. That deep discontent or anger that bubbles up at the slightest thing is trying to get your attention. It's asking you to take heed. Pay attention. Don't keep ignoring yourself. Don't dismiss **you**.

Since Scarlett's birth, I have given birth to my true self. Although I felt at the time that I had lost myself in the overwhelm of new mamahood, in hindsight I can see that I never really knew myself. I thought I did. I thought I had it all figured out. But the reality is that it is only through the years of births, babies and toddlers that I have glimpsed who I am at my core.

This is the gift of matrescence.

Dr Aurélie Athan describes matrescence as a deeply spiritual experience, and after coaching hundreds of mothers and connecting with thousands across the internet, I would agree. It **is** a spiritual experience.

In her research, Dr Athan found that 'Mothers described the lessons they learned as spurring a rebirth, as if they themselves were born, with new eyes, awakened to a reality of life which they had not known before.' She found, as I have from all my years of speaking to mamas, that the language new mothers used mirrored the terms we hear in spirituality: compassion, patience, surrender and divine love.

This is your spiritual journey. What you are feeling, what you are facing, what you are questioning, what you are discovering is your awakening.

The shame and guilt I felt after Scarlett's birth was my spiritual labour. It was the pain of my soul cracking open, and the disintegration of every single belief I had about myself. I thought that if I tried hard enough, studied more and asked the right people the right questions, I would be the perfect mother. I thought there was such a thing as a 'perfect mother'. And my darkest hour came when I realised that absolutely none of that was true, and all I could do was surrender. Surrender, then find compassion and patience for myself and connect with something more.

From that darkness came light. Just as those final centimetres of dilation are the most painful, before we are ready to push our baby into the world, so too are our own births as mothers. Those final lessons, those last few waves of hanging onto our deepest beliefs, are the most painful—the ones when our egos and willpower scream to be heard.

But we are being born. Just as in labour, the more you fear it, the harder and longer it will be. We are giving birth to a woman who is stronger, more empathetic, more spiritual and connected than she's ever been before. And she is magnificent!

CHAPTER 2

THE UNRAVELLING

The wound is the place where the light enters you.

— RUMI, PERSIAN POET

Think about this for a moment: we were never taught how to be a mama. Not a modern-day mother. We may have been hastily given breastfeeding advice and a quick tutorial on how to swaddle our squirming baby. But how to actually live as a modern-day mama and woman? No. We were just sent back into the wilderness of Instagram and comparisonitis on our own.

I also believe that we were never taught how to be a woman. Not in the true sense of how to honour our intuition and instincts; how to slow down and listen to our body; how to feel safe being soft and vulnerable; how to harness our compassion. Instead, we were taught how to climb the ladder, stand up to the boys, smash the glass ceiling, and do whatever we desired in this world. 'You can do whatever you put your mind to!'

Our own mothers and grandmothers wanted so much for us. They fought so long and hard for our rights to be doctors, lawyers and CEOs, that they overlooked our right to be soft, gentle, feminine women. They forgot to talk to us in quiet whispers about the sacred secrets of being a woman: how important it is to feel adored, to feel beautiful, to feel a deep connection to Mother Earth. To be cherished.

And so we pushed and pushed, chasing the goals we set as ambitious teenagers, never once considering that what we might really long for is a little bit of both.

From my earliest memories, I aspired to be a CEO, a journalist, a war correspondent. In my mind, there were shoulder pads (it was the 80s, after all), international flights, and rushing. Always rushing. Talking fast, walking fast, living fast. That's what most girls my age looked up to and admired.

So it's little wonder, really, that my addiction to busyness finally caught up with me. Ironically, after Scarlett's birth and that first stirring of the core question of matrescence (who am I now?), I began writing and researching about the transformation of motherhood. I settled on creating a blog about self-care for new mums. Every week, I would write about the power of meditation and mindfulness, interviewing leading self-help gurus from around the world. I would speak to experts like Louise Hay, Gabby Bernstein, Cheryl Richardson and Caroline Myss, nodding as they talked about these concepts, then post my interview and go back to the madness. No matter how many whispers the Universe was sending me, I steadily slipped back into superwoman mode.

I used to get such a buzz out of people saying, 'I don't know how you do it.' Like fuel for my insatiable ego, I would take on even more. Not even the surprise pregnancy of our little boy slowed me down—not one bit. I still juggled everything, including my 3.30am alarm for my job at the ABC, while solo parenting most days of the week. I was on autopilot. Whenever I felt overwhelmed, insecure or worried, I would go faster. Surely if I just worked harder and did **more**, things would get better? That's what I'd believed my whole life. That was the role modelling I'd had.

Slow down? No way. I could be who I wanted to be and be a mama to three! That 'inner split' that I'd felt when Scarlett was first placed on my chest just meant I needed to be more: I needed to straddle the roles of mother and journalist. Oh, plus wife, daughter, sister and friend.

But as Oprah says: *If you don't hear the whispers, the Universe will eventually scream at you.*

And scream the Universe did.

I was working on a top-rating breakfast radio show in Sydney, getting up at the now unimaginable time of 3.30am every single day, to go to work in the pitch black and create live radio. Breaking news, local stories, and the biggest challenge of all—making sure my presenter was happy, informed and ready. One of the best jobs in Radioland, and one I would have only dreamed about a few short years before, when I was slogging it out in regional South Australia.

But I was struggling. It reminded me of the film *The Devil Wears Prada* with Meryl Streep and Anne Hathaway, and the line everyone kept telling Anne's character, over and over: *A million girls would kill for that job.* A million journalists and producers would have killed for my job. And all I could think about was throwing it in and getting some freaking sleep.

For years, I missed waking my girls up in the morning. I wasn't there to get them dressed, or sort out breakfast requests, or kiss them goodbye at the day care or school door. My husband did all of that. Breakfast radio hours did mean that I was always there for afternoon pick-ups, but I was so exhausted that I felt like I was moving through mud. My husband was working in the world of Sydney advertising (think *Mad Men* without the perks), and was never home before 9pm. So I would be on my own with two girls under five every single day. Marque and I were like two solo parents at either end of the day; there were weeks when we didn't see each other from Monday to Thursday. And the girls' bedtime had to be my bedtime. In fact, if they weren't asleep and quiet by 7.05pm, Mean Mummy would come out. Again. I'd turn into this horrible ogre in an instant, yelling at them to go to sleep, so I could finally crash before doing it all over again. I just couldn't see past my daily alarm clock.

But I did have the job a million girls would die for.

It was at my nineteen-week scan for my little boy that the signs started to show something wasn't right. My cervix was thinner than it should be, I was told, and that could mean my baby would come early. Being a pushy journalist, I questioned their data and statistics, but agreed to come back in a week to check again. And I wasn't allowed to work in the meantime. This meant a week off, resting, to see if my cervix would bounce back after a little holiday from my life. But seven days later, it had thinned another five centimetres. My cervix was not holding up to holding my baby in.

I was prescribed progesterone cream, to be inserted internally every night. I hated it, and rejected the idea that there was anything wrong with me. Measuring the cervix was a new procedure, and therefore had never happened in my previous pregnancies. So who was to say that this wasn't normal for my body? I hadn't had a pre-term baby before, and I became obsessed with googling medical journals and data about cervix thickness and early labour. Arrogantly, I believed that I knew better than 'they' did. I was deep in denial that my lifestyle wasn't working, and I was determined to prove them all wrong.

By 24 weeks, it was obvious that the nightly progesterone cream was not doing what it should. While my cervix had only thinned by another two centimetres, the hope had been that it would stop altogether. One afternoon, straight after another long shift, I went to the hospital for yet another internal scan, to be met by the head of obstetrics. 'We think you need to stop work for four weeks', he told me, in a voice I imagined was usually used to portray news much more serious than mine. He calmly and clearly told me that my lifestyle was putting my baby at risk. 'It's obvious to us that your busy life is causing this thinning of your cervix; and because we can't change the fact that you have to look after two small children without any help, we have to change your working conditions. You need to stop work for four weeks.'

I couldn't believe it. My first reaction was, 'But it's a federal election, and I have to work!' I had proudly covered state and federal elections my whole career, producing election night coverage and coordinating interviews throughout the campaigns. They couldn't do it without me!

But the doctor insisted. We needed to get to the 'safe' mark of 28 weeks, which was the absolute minimum gestation for a baby to survive out of the womb.

I'm ashamed to say I rejected his advice. Yes, I stopped working, bursting into tears as I called my boss straight after the appointment. But I spent the following three days trying to get a second opinion. I paid for a one-off appointment with the top obstetrician in Sydney. While not totally agreeing with my doctor, he wouldn't risk telling me it wasn't necessary. I even called my midwife, who had been through my first two pregnancies and births, and cried to her about the injustice.

Of course I was concerned about the health of my unborn baby; but at the core of it, I hated the idea that my body was letting me down. I hated the idea that I had failed. I hated slowing down, saying I couldn't do it.

The four weeks passed very slowly. I spent a lot of time writing my blog and coming up with grand plans for my maternity leave: I'd write an ebook, I'd run a course, I'd do this and this and this. I pitched more articles to magazines and because I was doing it all from the comfort of my couch, I could justify my 'work'.

Exactly four weeks later, I walked back into ABC Breakfast Radio, right in the middle of the 2013 federal election campaign. And three days later, I went into labour.

I remember the exact moment it all started to fall apart. I had received a last-minute press release or explanation of something 'breaking' for the interview we were doing live on air. I hit print, jumped up, grabbed the paper off the printer, and looked down at my belly. 'Hang on buddy, we're going to run,' I said to my bump, then started running into the live studio to give the notes to the presenter. I think I even had heels on—always the professional (and a child of the 80s), high heels were a prerequisite. Even when pregnant and pre-dawn! And so I ran, feeling my unborn baby boy particularly—and strangely—low in my pelvis.

Just a few hours later, I started to feel funny. A weird pulling-down sensation, and (I would only share this with a fellow mama) I started to feel a let-down sensation in my breasts at the same time. I'd never, ever felt this before in my previous pregnancies, but I ignored it. However, over the next hour I noticed a bit of rhythm in the pulling-down sensation. 'What the hell is that?'

I thought. I was way over on the other side of Sydney at the time, my three-year-old daughter by my side, putting up posters for an upcoming workshop I was planning to run on post-natal support for new mothers (how ironic). I called the hospital, just in case. Of course, they told me to come in immediately, 'just to be safe'.

By the time we got to the hospital, I was having regular contractions. I walked up the hill to the entrance with tears in my eyes, dragging my daughter alongside as quickly as I could, repeating the prayer, 'Please stay in there, baby. Please, please stay in there.' I even started saying it out loud, as I rushed up the hill. 'Not now, little man. Not now, little man. **Please** stay in there.'

They admitted me straightaway, then called my husband at work. Monitors were put all over my belly, and it was confirmed that I was having contractions. I was given medication to try to slow the contractions down, and steroid injections to strengthen our little boy's lungs for when he was born. Our only hope was that I would be able to keep him inside for twelve hours, so I could have a second dose of steroids to help him breathe after birth.

The medication did seem to help, and things calmed down a little. Marque took our little girl home and was told he'd be called if anything happened. The muscle relaxants I'd been given made me drowsy and the steroids had given me a terrible headache, so I dozed. But around one in the morning, I was woken by more contractions.

This time they were really coming. Every three minutes. Even the midwife said, 'Wow, they're really happening now!'

Suddenly, my room was full. There was a visit from the neo-natal paediatrician and the head of the department. The prognosis for a baby born at 28 weeks wasn't the best—and he was small. I'd always had small babies, and this one was still tiny. Too tiny. I was told we needed a fighter. We'd been playing around with a few names before then, but at that moment it became clear that our little boy would be called Cassius. The first name of Muhammad Ali—our little fighter.

I kept asking if I should call my husband, but they kept telling me to wait and see. The contractions were certainly nothing like I'd experienced with the girls, but they were regular and building. More medication was administered, and another dose of steroids.

To this day, I am eternally grateful that it worked. Another hour later, my uterus stopped contracting and things slowed down again. My little boy was safe for the time being.

I spent five days in hospital, ensuring labour wouldn't start again. Five days in which I absolutely hit rock bottom in my superwoman world. I couldn't ignore it anymore—my crazy, busy, ambitious life had nearly brought our son into the world dangerously early. Enough was enough. Something had to change. It was obvious that if I was to keep this baby in, there would be no more work, no more workshops, and no more running between yoga class and school pick-ups.

It was time to slow down and figure out a new way of being.

When I was on that hospital bed, I downloaded my first chakra meditation. I asked one of my girlfriends to bring me some notebooks, and I poured my heart out into those journals. Why has this happened to me? What does this mean? Why have I been lying to myself and everyone else about how 'balanced' my life was? Why can't I be okay with slowing down and just being a mum?

But **how** was I going to be okay with slowing down and just being a mum?

Feminism has brought amazing benefits to many millions of women, but an unintentional side effect has been the supreme undervaluing of 'just' being a mother and a wife. Stay-at-home mums feel like they are always having to justify their worth, or explain why they're not working. And they often find themselves filling their lives up to look busy, because that's success, right?

Can I slow down and be 'just a mum'? This is the question so many of us ask. We feel a constant struggle within over being a mother and a woman. We want to be the best we can be, and we know it's a great blessing to be raising children. But we also want to be independent and successful. We want to be valued beyond motherhood.

But when you look back at the debate that has been raging since industrialisation (and beyond), it becomes obvious why we're struggling. The world around us has been arguing about what it takes to be a 'good woman and mother' since the dawn of modern time.

If we worked, we were judged. If we stayed home, we were judged. We were pitied, no matter what we chose: 'poor working mum missing out on so much' or 'poor stay-at-home mum, stuck in the kitchen and tied to the sink'.

This struggle is in our DNA. It's embedded into what we believe about motherhood and womanhood. Is it any wonder that we're so lost? That we don't know what to focus on? That we find ourselves trying to do it all, just in case that 'poor woman' judgement is cast?

It's not our fault we're struggling. Since we were little girls, we've been hearing a completely contradictory story of what we should aim for. So when faced with this inner split, we decide we need to just do it all.

Our generation has had an addiction to busyness, and I was a junkie. I could not slow myself down or stop my ambitious climbing up the ladder, even when my body screamed at me and I screamed at my family. When I was finally physically present with my girls, I could not slow my mind down long enough to be actually present with them, always checking Twitter for breaking news so I was on top of my job. I was looking for satisfaction, happiness and a feeling of being enough in all the wrong places.

As Sarah Napthali, guru of Buddhism for mothers, so beautifully puts it:

> *In our clearer moments we may glimpse what's going on—this endless pursuit of transitory happiness seems*

futile—but what can we do? Rather than acknowledge the inner deprivation, we try harder in the outer world because we obviously need more of what it can offer. We might convince ourselves we need a world trip, an affair or an exciting career change. And we're back in the cycle of demanding from the outside world.

But really, what we're searching for is within us.

Thank God, my cycle was finally coming to an end. My need for a daily 'fix' of busyness had been broken by sheer terror, and I was ready to rehabilitate. In whatever way I had to.

Cassius Kabbaz was finally born at 38 weeks. Exactly three days after I stopped the daily progesterone and was told I could finally get off the couch. I had spent ten weeks completely restricted; if I walked to the shops, that same pulling-down sensation would begin.

I had just three days of 'normal' life before my cervix let go. And in a dark and quiet room in the birthing centre, with just my husband and a midwife, I caught my little boy's head as he entered this world. And when I held him in my arms, I thanked him for already being my greatest teacher.

CHAPTER 3

TOWARDS AN ANSWER

Motherhood is a spiritual rite of passage, that in our society is commonly overlooked.

Have you considered the evolutionary leap your soul makes from going from maiden to mother?

— DR AURÉLIE ATHAN

Five years after Cass's birth, and eleven years into motherhood, I was walking the hallways of Columbia University. As a little girl, I had dreamed of studying and living in New York, like other little girls dream of being a ballerina or an actress. First New York, then the world, I thought. It was **the** dream. And there I finally was—trying hard not to ugly cry in the office of the leading global authority on the study of matrescence. And I was failing.

Eleven years of searching. Eleven years of trying to prove to myself and to everyone, especially my cynical media colleagues who thought I'd left the world of media to be a mummy blogger and life coach (whatever that meant), had come to an end. Finally, someone had the answer. And it wasn't just a spiritual 'woo-woo' answer; it was academic. Based on research. Finally, I had something I could anchor onto.

I had travelled across the globe and left my three babies at home, to sit in an office and hear: 'You were right, Amy. It is a thing. And it's called matrescence.'

The tears were instant and guttural. They came from all the doubt, self-judgement, resentment and anger. But they were also for all of you, the thousands of mamas who have shared your despair with me. I can feel you, all of you, as I write this. I feel the pressure we have been carrying and the guilt we heap on ourselves, because we believe there's something 'wrong' with us. And I feel for our children. If we had been given this knowledge, would it have been different?

I believe so. I truly believe that if we heal the mother, we heal the family. If we empower the mother to stop chasing this crazy, antiquated expectation of what she should be doing each day, then we will stop the yelling, the adrenal fatigue, the anxiety.

Matrescence is the emergence of a new identity—'the mother'—while trying to comprehend what happened to the old identity—'the woman'. It's that inner split I felt all those years ago, and it's the answer to why I ended up on that hospital bed in early labour.

It's the reason for it all. So why aren't we taught about this?

That was my question for Aurélie Athan in her office on that freezing cold New York winter day. Dr Athan is the new 'mother' of matrescence. As a psychologist based at Columbia University in New York, she struggled to find anything to explain the transition that women seemed to go through when they became mothers. She knew there was something there—she could hear it in the interviews she and her team conducted with mothers—but there was nothing in academia that could adequately explain it. That is, until she found the writings of another Columbia University-trained scholar by the name of Dana Raphael. Dana Raphael had coined the term 'matrescence' in the 1970s, to explain the complete transformation of the 'birth of the mother'. But it never really took off. (Interestingly, Dana Raphael was also the first to coin the term 'doula', which did gain popularity around the world.)

Dr Athan knew this was it; this was the framework she needed, to talk about what she was seeing and hearing in mothers. But it wasn't until a lengthy debate with her students one day, in which they tried to get a clear working description of what matrescence actually was, that 'matrescence, like adolescence' was born.

When I first heard the word 'matrescence' in a podcast, I had an instant, visceral reaction. There were instant tears. And as I began to share it with mamas around the world, their reaction was the same: tears, and then they'd say, 'This makes me feel so much less like a failure.' There has been such a huge reaction.

So why don't we know about this? Because, as I now understand, the world around us is still arguing about what it means to be a woman. Look around you—we're still trying to clarify our roles, what we should be doing, and how much we should be paid.

As Dr Catherine Birndorf, co-founder of The Motherhood Centre of New York (which focuses on holistic support for new mothers), said to me: 'If this had been men suffering for all these years, we would have whole universities dedicated to it.'

Dr Athan found some paper towel in the faculty kitchen to dry my tears. As she handed it to me she went on to say, 'Understanding that motherhood is the psychological and spiritual birth of a woman is the greatest story never told. It makes a tremendous difference. We can see in ancient cultures that we're meant to be handed down information as we move through these stages of life; those who have done it before need to pass down the knowledge to those who have yet to do it. That is the way this is meant to happen. And when it doesn't, when we don't have those markers or acknowledgements, we feel lost.'

She continued, 'It's also important to know that words create worlds. When we have a lack of language, and don't know how to articulate our experience and to put into words what we're feeling, it makes the process incredibly difficult. We need words to help heal. When we're feeling things that we don't know how to integrate and incorporate, we really feel torn apart and conflicted. We feel shame, isolation. So putting these things into words and having road maps saying that this is what you may experience is incredibly healing.'

What I have learnt since that day at Columbia has helped me put all this into context. It's allowed me to see things in perspective, gaining an insight into what our grandmothers faced, and then our mothers. And perspective is good; it shifts the lens from deep self-reflection (and judgement) to an awareness that most of what we are going through comes from what we've learned along the way. It's what we were handed down. It's what we've been taught.

We are here because it was decided, many years ago, that motherhood was not the sole purpose of womanhood, and a core group of phenomenally brave women blazed the path for us to get out of the home and into the workforce. In the late 1950s, women began to ask, 'Is this all?' Dive into the popular culture of the time, and you'll see that a woman's role was solely to have babies and make sure her husband was happy. She wasn't allowed to be interested in politics, and she certainly wasn't allowed to work. Despite a significant number of women gaining university education just a decade or two earlier, in the early fifties a woman was relegated to the home. Until … she broke.

By the end of the 1950s, doctors started reporting a massive increase in the number of anti-depressants prescribed for mothers. The reported number of women drinking increased too. Magazine and newspaper articles of the time began to report a rising dissatisfaction in marriages. The cracks were beginning to appear, eventually breaking down a whole system.

Suddenly, we were faced with the second wave of feminism. Women began returning to the workforce, and demand more than just babies and husbands. The younger generation burnt their bras and went on the pill. They went back to school and they challenged men for their rightful place at university and in the office.

Why is this important for us now? Remember, this was our mother's and grandmother's generation. These were the women who saw deep dissatisfaction in women forced to stay home. They knew what it felt like to be 'just a mum', and have no voice outside the home. They were the courageous warriors who allowed us to have freedom of choice now. But when they stepped into the office, they forgot to tell us how to be a mother.

Work was where we were respected. The workforce was where we could find our power. And in a way, the value of motherhood was discarded. We stopped having babies, or delayed it for as long as we could. IVF and infertility rates skyrocketed, as we suddenly realised that maybe we did want this thing called motherhood after all. But how we actually 'do it all'? Well, that's where superwoman comes in.

Is it any wonder we carry such wounds around these roles? Think about it for a moment:

> What does being a mother mean to you?
> What does being a wife, a partner, mean?
> What views do you carry deep within you, about working part-time, or changing your ambition for your children?

> How do you feel about staying at home while your partner works? Does it feel empowering or completely disempowering?

> What deep judgement do you carry about choosing your career advancement over being at school pick-up every single day?

Matrescence is not just about becoming a mother—it's about a complete transformation in all areas of your life. As Dr Athan says: 'The fact is, we're always thinking about our children, and we have to start seeing the experience through the transformation of the woman. Our children really are the drivers of human development. We typically only think about our influence on them, but they have a great deal of influence on us. They are the teacher.'

But without an understanding of how and why this happens, we will continue to burn out and feel completely lost. Our rates of post-natal depression and anxiety will continue to rise; our relationships will continue to fall apart; our bodies will continue to break; and the way we mother our children will continue to suffer.

It's not your fault if you find this confronting and scary, nor is it a sign that you are failing. You have just been caught up in a system that has been rigged, right from the beginning.

But this is my invitation, mama! This is my invitation to you to come on an exploration of all you have been told, and all you carry deep within your cells, about what it means to be a woman and a mama. This is my invitation to redefine it in your own way, free from the antiquated beliefs of the past.

As Dr Birndorf, co-founder of The Motherhood Centre, describes it: 'We need to acknowledge that the feeling women are having around this is legitimate. It has meaning and value and has to be accepted. It's a normal, typical process. If I could, I would tell the mother that she can say, without excuse and without apology, "I am a mother now, and I need to focus on what that means." She needs to be able to consider this transition as the primary transition, and that all the other identities need to be reconsidered: partner, colleague, sister, daughter, friend, woman.'

On reflection, motherhood stirred something in me, but I ignored it. I pushed past it, going back to my old beliefs of what my life should look like. Even though my body and spirit were calling for me to abandon this endless pursuit of success, my mind was so attached to the ideal, I ignored it. Until I couldn't anymore.

Don't let the stirrings go unnoticed in your life any longer. What you're feeling is real—and it's important. Notice it. Feel into it. Don't push past the depression, the anxiety, the overwhelm, the broken body, in pursuit of an outdated version of what we should be doing.

Be here with it now. And know that you are on the edge of something magnificent.

But **how**, you ask? How do I take the first steps to wholeness, to the rebirthing that is happening?

You start with kindness. Deep self-compassion at soul level. Compassion from knowing that this is more than just your experience of motherhood—it is the collective. And then you begin to reframe everything you know about yourself: your strengths, your belief in yourself, your value as a woman, your grace and beauty, and your relationships.

Walk with me. Come on this exploration with me. Let's crack open what we've been told about being a 'good mother' and a 'good girl', and redefine it for ourselves. We have to—we can't have another generation of women sick, burnt out and yelling at everyone. We can't let misconceptions of what it means to be a whole woman keep us chained to overachievement.

In the coming chapters, I will share with you the six areas that I have found help us move through this transformation with ease and grace. These are the areas I've had to look at in my own life, to heal and transform, and what I have shared with the thousands of mamas who have been a part of my journey. It's a simple formula of self-discovery, of looking within yourself and seeing what emerges.

Scattered among my insights and the stories of many of the mamas I have coached, I also share some of the most important and insightful interviews I have conducted during the past decade. Each interview brings its own insight into matrescence, grace, motherhood and womanhood. Each one highlights a new way of looking at what you're feeling, and what you're going through.

Be gentle with yourself as you move through this. Take your time, and acknowledge all that comes up. After coaching hundreds of women through this process, I know for sure that underneath the mask of motherhood, there is often a lot of very raw emotion waiting to be released. In my workshops, mothers often start to cry as soon as they begin to introduce themselves. We are all just barely holding on, and as soon as we're given a little space and support, raw emotion spills out.

Know that this is part of the process. But you're here now, and ready.

Let's try new ways of thinking, and let's no longer hide. It's what motherhood is here to teach you.

Serious transformations begin with two commitments: the courage to try new things and act in new ways; and the honesty needed to no longer hide from or lie to ourselves.

YUNG PUEBLO

CHAPTER 4

FOCUS ONE > KINDNESS

Be gentle first with yourself, if you wish to be gentle
with others.

— LAMA YESHE

Just imagine for a moment that we thought about the process of
becoming a mother completely differently. Let's just play a game
of pretend for a second.

Imagine we lived in a world where women were honoured
for their ability to create life. A world in which we were seen as
the source of life, the creators, the ones who held the future in
their hands. Imagine if we knew that in the process of becoming
a mother, a woman was finally stepping into her full power; she
was awakening to herself, to her ability and her strength.

And yet, she was meticulously trained and initiated into this
new phase of her being. She was nurtured, taken into circle with
other older mothers, and told what was coming. She was spoken
to about the many paths it takes to become 'the mother'—the

conception, the birth, the first months, the struggles, the triumphs. But she was reassured, with her hands held and soft eyes looking into hers, that her way was the right way for her.

Imagine she was supported to understand her baby, and then her toddler and her child. But at every milestone, she was reminded that this was a new beginning for her too. She was brought back into circle, to be given the space to reflect, to see how she was changing, and to ask herself what she needed now.

Imagine she was told it's going to get bumpy—because all transformations must contain a cycle of destruction and rebirth. But she was safe; it was part of the process. In fact, it was the best bit. It was the part that was going to crack her open and expose her true grit and beauty. She was going to emerge from it whole, free from what she used to think was important, free from the attachment to all that she thought she was.

She will be wise, and intuitive, and powerful. She will be whole.

Imagine a world that looked upon what a mother does each day and marvelled—as she rocks the baby and soothes the toddler and whispers in the night to quieten frightened minds. A world that celebrated her. Honoured her. Because everyone believed that there was no greater role. Just imagine.

> Can you feel how much kinder you'd be on yourself?
> Can you see that it is actually not your fault that it feels this hard, and this dark?

> Can you see that the problem is that no-one has ever honoured what you're going through, reassured you that all is okay, and reminded you that you're in the middle of one of the greatest evolutions of all?

So let's just start there. Let's start from a place of compassion. A place that acknowledges that you've been trying to figure this whole thing out without having a clue of what you're actually meant to be figuring out. It's like you're in the middle of a horror film, running around trying to get out, without realising that the whole thing has been made up by other people decades ago.

Traditionally, we would gather in circles, surrounded by the elders, with their wisdom and understanding. We would have heard their stories of matrescence, of that beautiful season of life we were about to enter. We would have been made to feel that it was normal, just part of the process. We would have heard stories of similar struggles, almost laughing as we finally saw the truth: that we're all just figuring it out.

And so, with the understanding that this was part of the path, we would forgive ourselves. Once the whispers of the transition to motherhood had been shared, we would know that we are no different to the women we most admire, and we would have softened. Forgiven ourselves. Lightened up about it all, and smiled at the growth we were witnessing.

We would have heard our own inner voice say, 'It's okay. You're just learning.'

In all cultures we have transitions. Like adolescence, where we celebrate the fact that the 'old' you is gone, but you are becoming someone so much better. And it's these initiations and ceremonies and the handing over of wisdom—such a beautiful process—that we have wiped from our lives as women right now. Just as we should celebrate the start of menstruation with our young teenage girls, so too should the start of motherhood be surrounded by ritual and ceremony.

When I first heard about matrescence, I cried and cried. But then I was angry. I still am. Because after years of talking to and coaching thousands of mamas stuck in the middle of a bad dream out of their control, I can see that most of our pain comes from our judgement of ourselves. It comes from our belief that we 'should have this figured out'.

Most of the time, we think it's the kids we need to figure out. It's the act of mothering. If only we could get the routine right, or the food right, or the bedtime right, we'd nail it. Then, it would all stop being so hard, and we'd be okay again. But children never stop evolving, which means the 'problem' we're trying to fix never stops evolving either.

And so we never stop judging and searching. That's why matrescence can never be about where you are in relation to where you child is—it has to be all about you. It's in how you feel about yourself, and how you judge yourself. And to move out of the darkness and into the light of transformation, we have to understand how to turn our mean inner voice around.

> The Inner Mean Mama

I call it the Inner Mean Mama. That voice that says you're doing it all wrong. It was the voice that plagued me, day in and day out, when I first became a mother. And it still appears in my moments of fear. When I allow the perfectionist within to take over, and let my comparison with others become louder than my faith, she comes back. Nastier than ever. It has taken me a long time to learn how to recognise her, but I do. I know her tricks. I know how to face her with fierce courage now.

But oh, that Inner Mean Mama is mean. She is awful, toxic, nasty. I have worked with mamas whose internal dialogue was so mean, they couldn't even say the words out loud. Judgement, hate, guilt. It's all there. When I have gently encouraged them to share what their inner voice is saying, they can't. They know it's too awful. And yet, they believe it. Somewhere inside, it feels like truth to them.

This is why this whole journey must begin with kindness. If there was one element that runs through every spiritual philosophy, every self-help book, and every yoga class I've ever attended, it would be this:

Kindness. Self-compassion. Treating yourself gently. Being your own best friend.

Not that that is an easy thing to grasp. Never before have we had to mother—and live—so publicly. Moments that would have been deeply private in the past are now willingly shared on social media. Even if you've decided not to be one of 'those' mamas who put a flattering filter over every family moment, I bet you're still finding it hard to block out the comparison of everyone else's highlight reel.

Have you ever found yourself viewing your children through the lens of Instagram? Or moved things around in your home before taking a picture, so it's Facebook-worthy? It sounds crazy, doesn't it? This obsession over how others view our inner world is toxic. And it's causing us to chase something that will never ever make us happy.

We have lost the ability to listen to our own wisdom, and treat ourselves like we would our best friend. We have completely disconnected from our true self, so we go searching for anything that feels a little like connection in the form of our phones. But what we are really aching for is a connection to ourselves.

How do you speak to yourself? When you are quiet, and tune into your inner dialogue, what are you telling yourself?

Silence can feel scary. Trying to be in the moment can be confronting, when the voice that rises up is so mean. One mama told me she reaches for her phone, because when she just tries to sit with her baby and toddler on the floor to play, she realises how lonely she is. She lost both her parents before she became a parent, and she felt completely isolated from her friends and community. Every time she was quiet, there was the voice: lonely, sad, angry. And so her phone was her escape. It gave her the connection she was craving, or so she thought.

Avoidance can feel easier. But it's not. When that mama really looked at it, it was making the pain worse. Instead of numbing herself with social media, it was time to practise self-compassion.

Matrescence brings us right to the edge of the parts of us that we might not like. It shines a light on our unresolved grief, our old pain around the way we were parented, or our underlying fear that our partner doesn't really love us. This is not just about how we parent our children—it's about how we reparent ourselves. This is the beautiful healing opportunity of mamahood.

However, the only way to heal is by starting with kindness.

I know that you know compassion. And I know you know kindness. I know because you are a mama, and you have felt a deep, deep understanding and forgiveness for your little one at some stage, when they were struggling. When they have been sick, or when they have hurt themselves, or when they've been so overtired they can't think straight and even the slightest change in their world causes a meltdown. So many times, I've seen a mama drop down to their child's level with empathy to soothe a frazzled little mind. It's what we do.

You know compassion; now you just have to turn it around to shine back on yourself. As the Buddha said:

If your compassion does not include yourself, then you are not complete.

Self-compassion is about looking upon yourself as you would your child or a loved one, and treating yourself in the same way.

Dr Kristin Neff is a pioneer in the research and teachings of self-compassion. This is how she describes it: 'Compassion has three basic components: noticing suffering, being kind and caring in response to that suffering, and then remembering imperfection is part of the human experience.'

When it comes to women, harsh judgement of ourselves is often closely tied to perfectionism. We hold such high standards for ourselves, and expect so much of ourselves, that when we fall short of that standard, we're certain we have failed. And boy, do we have a lot of standards to meet in our world!

Perfect house, perfect body, perfect children. But at what cost? How is that making you feel? What are you missing out on because of this pursuit of perfection?

We will not be another generation of women who are forced to conform to external masculine ideas of what is valuable. We won't. We will bring deep self-compassion to ourselves as we awaken and transform. We will notice our suffering; we will be kind and caring to ourselves in response to that suffering; and then we will remember that as we rise and find ourselves again, we will not be perfect. It will be messy at times, but we are clear now—**we will value what we are doing as mothers**.

There's a scene in *Eat Pray Love* that I have acted out in my own life far too many times. Elizabeth Gilbert is desperate and lost in the middle of her marriage and wondering what to do. When she wakes in the middle of the night, she drops to her knees in the bathroom and calls out to God, 'What should I do?'

She sobs, 'What am I supposed to do now?' And while there on her knees, a voice as clear as if someone was standing next to her replies, 'Go back to bed.'

I believe this is what God would say to most overwrought mothers too.

I have dropped to my knees in desperation, sometimes hidden in the bathroom while crying children tapped on the door looking for me. At other times in the middle of the night, as dark thoughts of fear have overtaken me, I've asked the Creator a very similar question: 'What should I do? I don't know what to do anymore. I don't know how to do this. Please help me. Please show me.'

And I swear, the same God that spoke to Liz Gilbert has answered me too: 'Go back to bed, Amy. Get some sleep. You'll be okay.'

Over years of coaching thousands of women, I feel my role has been similar to this voice of the night. I have sat, listening to and reading hundreds and hundreds of similar cries for help. Questions of despair, begging to understand how to do it better, how to not feel so lost and scared. And as I listened, nodded, tears in my eyes as I felt their pain, I've found myself saying …

You just need some sleep, beautiful. You're just trying to figure this out. You're changing; this is all new. But I promise you, it's going to be okay. You've got this. Just rest, and you'll be okay.

This is how I wish you spoke to yourself.

Think again of the love you have for your child. Not the happy moment love bubble that consumes you when you watch them sleep, but the unconditional love that sustains you through the times of button-pushing that children inevitably bring.

A mother's love is unconditional. A mother can see the good beneath their child's behaviour, no matter what. She has the innate ability to look beyond the tantrum, the tears, the biting and the hitting, to see that her child is beautiful, but struggling. She sees they are tired, or overwhelmed, or scared. They are drowning in the changes in their life. They are growing.

A mother can see that the outward behaviour is just a manifestation of the struggles within. In fact, she is often the only one who sees beyond the actions, and knows the truth—her children simply need comfort and support. A safe space to feel their feelings. Love, no matter what. She knows that's when their true divine selves will emerge again.

I long for you to have an Inner Voice of deep compassion, beautiful mama. I long for you to feel this about yourself. But I know it can feel strange at first. Kindness can feel very foreign, when you're riddled with shame. I know. When you feel you need to hide parts of yourself and your feelings, finding that Inner Voice of compassion can be near impossible. It can turn into a bit of a tug of war between your best self and your very worst self:

It's okay, you're doing the best you can.

*No you're not! You're lazy and you never get it right. You
always screw it up. And now you're going to screw your
children up too.*

Sometimes, the ego voice can be an exceptional debating partner.
The evidence it has on you is immense, and it is ready and willing
to hurl it at you at any given moment. Talk about hit you when
you're down—this is the Inner Mean Mama's signature move!

Many years ago, I began to see this toxic pattern in my own
thinking. I would do something I wasn't proud of—yell at one of
my kids, forget something important and beat myself up for not
being organised, look at someone else 'nailing it' and compare
myself—and the first thoughts would begin. 'See!' I would hear.
'See! You can't be a mindfulness coach/are never on top of things/
are never going to catch up and be a success'. It would be just a
sentence or two at first, a little poking of the bear. But I'd react. I'd
bite. I'd take that open invitation of negativity and dive right in.
And pretty soon, it was more than just that moment I'd messed
up—it was everything. All of the times I'd yelled or gotten it
'wrong' would come out, and I would spiral down into the depths
of despair.

Thoughts have energy. What you think has power. And if
you take the bait, and follow the breadcrumbs, you'll end up in
a world of pain. It's just how it works.

The key is to not take those first crumbs. That's it, mamas.
We have to practise, over and over again, a way to hear that voice,

acknowledge that it's back, then drop it. And come back with kindness.

During meditation many years ago, I remember hearing a description of thoughts being compared to clouds passing through the sky; you see them, but you let them just float past. Apparently, it's meant to help deal with all those random thoughts that pop into our mind when you're trying to be zen.

I like to use this analogy for the Inner Mean Mama too: hear it, know what it is (naming it as the Inner Mean Mama voice is very powerful), and then let it slide past you. In other words, don't give it power.

It isn't your truth. It's the voice of a tired, angry, overwhelmed woman in the middle of a massive transformation in her life, trying to also help a tiny human being or two through their own transformation.

Don't give it any power. Instead, come back to that compassion. Remember, you are becoming new.

> Self-compassion for the Inner Mean Mama

Sarah Napthali is one of the most inspiring mamas I've ever met. Her books on Buddhism and motherhood not only changed my life, but the lives of thousands and thousands of mamas around the world. Her unique ability to bring Buddhist principles into motherhood has been the cornerstone of my understanding of compassion in matrescence.

'When a woman becomes a mother, it's potentially a very stressful time, because everything she thought she was and all the things that gave her life structure are ripped out from under her,' she told me. 'She is faced with isolation, she's at the beck and call of her baby, or she's got toddlers interrupting every conversation. In my case, I had a toddler who was always running away and it felt like I was just chasing him for a couple of years. At social gatherings, I couldn't even participate because I was always running! There can be a lot of frustration at all the drudgery.'

Sarah continued, 'Self-compassion is one of the very first things we need to learn as mothers, and as women. It can be a bit dangerous when you first start watching your thoughts and you're actually shocked by how self-absorbed you are, or how mean you are, or how angry or cranky you are. And you could start to just really hate yourself and, even if you start to meditate, then you're actually just meditating to change yourself because you hate yourself.

'You've got to meditate from a place of self-acceptance. I accept myself, I love myself, warts and all. And if you've got that attitude, then you've got the guts to look deeper. If you hate yourself, then you'll be scared to look deeper at the murky stuff that you're going to find. But with self-compassion—the kind of compassion that you have for your children when they err—if you can apply that to yourself, I really think it's a good way of pressing the accelerator on your practice. Mother the mother. Take inspiration from that unconditional love you have for your children. You can forgive them anything and you can get over anything they have done; so do that for yourself as well.'

When I first began, I know I was doing this out of a place of deep self-judgement and the desire to change. I felt I had to, if I was ever going to be the mother and the woman I wanted to be. But the underlying desire was to change—not to accept. That is the difference.

To look upon ourselves and where we are right now, even with all the messiness, and say, 'That's okay. You're learning. You're doing a great job.' That's true kindness.

> It's okay not to love it

She sits down in the circle, and I can already see tears welling behind her eyes. As each mama introduces herself and shares why she's there, I can feel her apprehension about speaking. She's afraid of what might come out. But eventually it's her turn, and the words spill out along with her tears. 'I thought it would be different. I wanted to be a mother so badly—it took us seven rounds of IVF and three miscarriages to get here. But now … it's just so hard.'

And then, the apologies: 'Sorry. I shouldn't be crying. I love being a mama. Sorry.'

The guilt and the shame. The judgement of not 'loving it all'. The tug of war within that comes from wanting something so badly and then wondering if it is really all worth it. Why are we so afraid of sharing what we really feel? Judgement. The deep fear of judgement.

This mama went on to tell me later that she distinctly remembers making a deal with God. As another round of IVF began, after another devastating miscarriage, she remembers trying to negotiate a baby with whatever Universal Force was up there. *If I get this baby, I promise I will be the most loving mother ever. I will give it everything, and all of me. I will love it more than any mother has ever loved a child.*

So when she found herself not loving it all, she felt like a failure. And a fraud.

Where did we get this crazy idea that we must surrender all of ourselves to the needs of our children? When did being a 'good' mother mean we were never allowed to whisper our desire for our old lives?

Motherhood can bring a lot of grief. We don't talk about it much, because there seems to be so much shame around it, but there isn't a mother in the world who doesn't have her moments of longing for her 'old' life. She feels that split within—the old and the new—and there are times she secretly wonders whether it really was the right 'choice'.

Does that make you a bad mum? No, it makes you real. And it shows me you're in the middle of the transformation of matrescence.

To become anew we must leave the old behind. This should have been part of what you were told. I should have been able to gather you into the circle, like I did with that mama that day (and so many others), to give you a chance to speak, to share, to cry all those tears—without judgement. And given you the assurance that we all feel the same.

What parts of your old life and self are you grieving? It's okay to admit it. In fact, it's part of the transformation.

There has to be a shedding. There will be old parts of your life, old patterns of thinking, people you've known for a long time who will fall away. That's part of the process. Be kind to yourself as you move through this stage; remind yourself daily that everything is happening for a reason. And that you will emerge on the other side wiser, more powerful, more whole.

And you don't have to love it all. Truly, you don't. When that beautiful mama realised that it was okay to have wanted her child for so long and yet still wish for her old life at times, her whole body shifted. She became lighter, right before our eyes. The heaviness of the shame of losing her temper at the child she had wished for was finally lifted. And when I checked in with her a little while later, she told me the anger she felt had gone too.

No longer did she snap in frustration, because the voice in her head was softer. She didn't yell, because her mind wasn't yelling at her.

It always, always starts with our inner voice. If you can find a way to treat yourself kindly, and remind yourself you absolutely do not have to love all of this (no-one does), then everything else will come from kindness too.

Part of the reason we grieve is because we believe it's gone forever. We believe that the carefree, spontaneous, ambitious, passionate woman is gone forever. And in part, that's true. That version of that women will not return—there is no going backwards in life. But please trust me when I say that's not the end of your story. The whole point of this divine transformation of matrescence is that you will emerge whole again, but with a whole new wholeness. You thought you were whole before, completely unaware of a dormant power waiting inside you. You thought that was your power, but it was not. It was a false power in the acceptance of others' ideals and the pursuit of success. It was not your truth. And when, through this process, that awareness finally awakens within you, you will realise that you were never really whole at all.

I thought I was whole—but mamahood showed me that at my core, I didn't like who I was. I felt I had to prove myself to be loved. Now, with the gift of matrescence, I have found a woman who loves herself. She accepts herself with grace and compassion. When she falls down now, she lovingly reaches out a hand and says, 'It's okay. You've got this.'

So be kind. Look upon yourself with Mother Eyes. See that you've been scared and navigating in the dark, and that no-one has been holding your hand or whispering to you in the dark, telling you all is okay. No-one has been gathering around you, to show you the path ahead and remind you that this is all part of it. Until now.

My Inner Mean Mama has finally subsided. I've become so familiar with her, I can recognise her very first whispers. But it's taken such commitment. I have had to work on reprogramming that endless mean voice over and over again. And replace it with compassion.

I started small, with small wins throughout my day. I trained myself to start seeking out the little moments I did well, the ones I was proud of. Rather than replaying all the failures through my head at the end of the day, I purposefully chose to hone in on the good bits. It worked.

A lot of the mamas I have shared this exercise with have really struggled with this though. The idea of reflecting on what we are really good at is too daunting; it only makes them feel less adequate, as they realise they don't feel very proud of many things anymore. They're so used to self-judgement and endless guilt, switching to positive is a leap too far.

But I find that most of them are overlooking the most basic (and important) things they are already doing. Like cuddles. Like knowing how to comfort a sick child. Like baking muffins, singing in the car, being a supportive friend, or remembering people's birthdays. The tiny moments that make them a great friend, mama, partner, daughter, woman.

One beautiful mama once sent me an email, outlining all the things she thought she was doing wrong and all the ways she was failing as a mother and wife. She told me she could hardly see the screen she was crying so much. She felt so lost and was desperate to change.

After lovingly telling her that she was amazing to even be declaring that enough was enough and it was time to change, I asked her to send me back her answers to the questions: what are you great at, and what do you like about yourself. 'I know it's hard,' I told her. 'Just start with the smallest things.'

This was her response:

> I'm finding it really hard to find things I'm 'great' at and that I 'like' about myself, but here goes …
>
> I'm great at reading books to my girls. I'm quite animated in my delivery and it's enjoyable for us all.
>
> I'm good at encouraging and supporting others.
>
> I'm good at verbalising my feelings.
>
> I'm good at handstands.
>
> I'm good at finding things in the dark, i.e. if something has been dropped, I can find it.
>
> I'm good at hearing a noise in the middle of the night and determining where it came from.

And that's how we start. Every time that mama finds something in the dark, or reads to her children in a big bear voice, or does a handstand, she's going to reflect on this. She's going to feel stronger, and prouder. She's going to recognise that this is her special thing for her family, and start to feel better about herself.

Find the small things and go from there. Some of the negative mantras of our Inner Mean Mama have been embedded in our brains for most of our lives. They are the words we've been listening to for decades. A bad earworm that is on repeat, day in and day out.

So don't be hard on yourself, if your default mantra is pretty mean. If you catch the negativity on high rotation in your mind, simply start by giving it a little wave saying, 'Oh hi! You're back. I know you. But I don't believe you anymore.'

As Pam Grout so beautifully explains in her book *E-Squared*, changing our thoughts is like toilet training a puppy: every time we find the puppy peeing behind the couch, we pick it up and take it outside to a tree. Pick it up and show it the tree. Over and over again. And one day, the puppy will just go to the tree.

Our thoughts are no different. Pick them up, and show them the tree. Before we know it, they'll wander out to that tree all on their own.

In Sarah Napthali's words:

> *Self-compassion has been the greatest lesson of all for me. That's definitely the real cornerstone of my practice, because there's just so much potential for feelings of guilt and shame and inadequacy. Sometimes I actually do it physically. I just take my right hand and give my left arm a little rub— the way you comfort a child who's upset. And that sort of human touch releases oxytocin in the brain. Babies need that*

reassuring touch of another human being to feel soothed, and we can apply that to ourselves. And if I am in a meeting or I am at work and I can't give my arm a rub because I'll look like a weirdo, I do it mentally because the brain doesn't know the difference. You can get that little oxytocin squirt whether you do it mentally or physically or sitting in meditation. Just think about giving yourself a hug or the kind of reassurance that you'd give a small vulnerable child.

KINDNESS ACTIVITY > Pay Attention To What You're Paying Attention To

Taming that Inner Mean Mama and recognising that you are doing the very best you can is a learnt skill. It's something we have to commit to, over and over again, if we are to rise up from matrescence with grace. But we have to commit to this change from a place of love, not fear or hate. We have to find a way to look at ourselves and fully love and accept who we are right now; then from that place, commit to what we most want.

Can you see the difference? Can you see how different that would feel—to show up for yourself each day out of love and respect?

One of the best ways I have seen this work with many hundreds of mamas is to get them to practise paying attention to what they're paying attention to. In other words, spend time each day celebrating what they are doing well.

At the end of the day, either lying in bed or sitting with a journal, write down five things that you are proud of having done that day. This can be tough at first. Learning to hear how you speak to yourself can be quite confronting.

One mama shared with me as she embarked on this exact exercise, 'This is going to be challenging for me. When I stop and listen, I can hear so much negative talk inside me—so much berating and harshness and not forgiving. I have trained myself for many years to be this way, and it is so sad that I have felt like I needed to treat myself like this. I would be devastated if my kids felt this way about themselves. I love the idea of writing five things I love about myself or what I did well each day, and how this might start to change my thinking.'

One step at a time. One moment at a time. As I explained to this beautiful mama, that voice is not you. It's an overwhelmed, scared programmed way of thinking that has been passed down to you. It's not your truth.

CHAPTER 5

FOCUS TWO > **STRENGTH**

I hope you will go out and let stories, that is life, happen to you, and that you will work with these stories ... water them with your blood and tears and your laughter till they bloom, till you yourself burst into bloom.

— CLARISSA PINKOLA ESTES

Strength is masculine. At least, that's what we've been taught.

For thousands of years, we have been relegated to the bottom of the pile, told that we are sensitive, weak, emotional, vulnerable. We were told we needed a protector, and then we were told not to rely on a protector, but instead to learn to protect ourselves— because at the core of it, we were defenceless little things.

And so, generation after generation of women before us viewed strength as something outside of themselves. Something foreign they had to fight for. Certainly not something that came naturally, or from their deep inner wisdom.

I spent years of my life believing I wasn't strong. I would set goals, promise myself that I'd never do something again—only to give up and give in. I have diary upon diary from my teenage years filled with 'from tomorrow onwards I will not ...', followed by another entry beating myself up because I didn't stick to what I said I would. I equated willpower with strength, and therefore thought I didn't have either of them.

I did not think I was strong as a mama. I didn't make it through labour without an epidural; I couldn't cope with the endless sleepless nights; and I crumbled at the idea of just being home with an unhappy baby, day after day. I also deeply believed that I wasn't strong because I couldn't say 'no' to that extra glass of wine when I was out, always going too far and feeling ashamed the next day.

Weak. No willpower. No determination.

When we feel a deep inadequacy within, we pour all of our attention into trying to 'fix it', which is exactly what I did. I spent my life trying to prove that I was strong.

I didn't need a man, I didn't need your help, I didn't need anyone, thank you very much. The walls around my heart were so impenetrable that even I didn't know what was behind them. I'd spent my life trying to live up to this unreal expectation of what a strong, successful woman 'looked' like. So I didn't even know my real self—which was actually an emotionally sensitive, deep thinking, deeply spiritual girl. But that didn't fit the mould, so it was pushed to one side. Over and over again.

The reason we don't believe we are strong is because we have the wrong definition of it. We think strength is someone else— that woman who never yells, is always solid and strong, and is clear on what she needs to do and when.

Deep in our core belief system, strength is a masculine quality. It's determination, commitment, solidity. It's climbing the ladder, smashing the walls in front of us, and kicking goals. Once again, it is all masculine.

We don't value the strength it takes to nurse a child every few hours a night for months on end, because a) we think we're crap at it, and b) no-one says, 'Wow, look how strong that woman is, she is a mother!' Nor do we value the sheer tenacity and strength it takes to juggle the needs of so many others, to the detriment of our own.

Let's be honest here for a moment: my husband would not be able to do what I do. He does not know the first thing about what needs to go to school on which day, which bills are paid from which account, or what the kids are going to get for their birthdays. I love my husband deeply and I have come to a profound understanding that he is the perfect guy for me. But most of the time, his children's birthdays come around as a bit of a surprise each year. And he is almost always seeing the Christmas presents for the first time when the children do. He can't do what I do. He just can't.

But do I look at what I do every single day and say, 'Wow, girl! You are so strong to do all of this, day in and day out'? Nope. Most of us don't.

Let's pause for a moment and get something really, really clear. **You are strong because you are a mother.**

You don't need any other evidence. You don't need a list of 'how I got through this' or 'I know I am strong because' (although that helps silence the Inner Mean Mama). All you need to accept, on the deepest level possible, is that you did it. You are doing it. The hardest job in the world. And nothing makes you stronger.

When we start to connect to the idea of true strength, and how we always have it at our disposal, we start to view ourselves in a different light. We start to see the warrior we really are. We start to connect to that inner goddess (yes, goddess) who is always there, waiting for us to call on her.

Yogi Bhajan was the man responsible for bringing the teachings of Kundalini yoga to the West. Before that, it was a secret philosophy, shared only among the highest level of yoga teachers in India. But in the 70s, Yogi Bhajan saw what was happening in the West—how we were headed for self-destruction and depression—so he decided to take Kundalini to the United States, to start to share this science. And in his teachings, women— mothers in particular—are honoured as the true powerhouses and leaders.

When speaking about mothers, Yogi Bhajan said: 'You are the nucleus of this Universe. You are the source of beginning. You are the master of the space. You are the hub, you are the pivot, you are the force, you are the mother. If you walk tall, that's all you have to do. Resurrect yourself, exalt yourself, excel. You are born to rule; that's the rule of creation.'

Let me break that down:

You are the nucleus of the Universe—in other words, you are the centre of it all.

You are the source of the beginning—you are where life begins.

You are the master of the space. As mamas, you are the hub; we know this, right? We are the masters of the space in our homes and in our families. We are the hub of it all.

You are the pivot—I love this one. Yes, it is us that pivots our family's emotions, turns the day around, changes a mood with a simple touch.

You are the force—yes! When we are clear and strong, we are.

You are the mother.

And if you walk tall, that's all you have to do. Resurrect yourself—find yourself again, mama.

Here's what I think is the source of so much disconnect from our power and strength as women—and the source of so much pain: we have let our power be taken away, and often at the very beginning of our journey as a mother.

Becoming a mother is meant to be the most sacred time in our lives. It's meant to be our connection to the divine feminine—a nine-month journey of soul-level spiritual awakening, when we begin to grow another life in us and become a true creator. But modern-day motherhood is rarely that.

Pregnancy is overmanaged. We are prodded and poked and measured and tested. We are disconnected from the wisdom and wonder of our body, and filled with fear and statistics. And what if we don't just fall pregnant naturally, one beautiful Sunday evening when all the stars align? Then we have failed before we have even begun. There's something unwomanly about us. We're broken.

Once again, our power is taken away. We disconnect from ourselves as women. We doubt ourselves.

There are very few women in this world who are happy with the way they birthed their babies. Some wish things could have been slightly different, while others hold deep pain and grief about the process. Our medical system has taken life-changing and lifesaving modern procedures, that we desperately need in some circumstances, and turned them into a disempowering intervention. Even when we need these miracle procedures to save us and our babies' lives, we don't feel empowered by that choice. We feel shamed, or sad, or that we've failed.

Enough.

Enough of the judgement of how you did it and how she did it. Enough of the disempowerment of new mothers. The only difference between an empowering birth and a grief-ridden one is the mother's feelings of being heard and involved. That's where her strength comes from. And if she has that strength—my God, she can get through anything!

Dr Birndorf has seen what real strength is. At The Motherhood Centre of New York, she regularly sees mamas struggling with post-natal depression, post-natal anxiety, and the intensity of the transition to matrescence. But when you hear what she has to say about the strength of a mama, your eyes will fill with tears: 'It's so interesting what you see wake up in a woman when motherhood begins. It wakes up this feeling of wanting to do right by her children. She may have been able to ignore parts of her life and herself when it was just her; but now, she knows she needs to do something about it. There is such strength in every mum—and given the opportunity, they will run far and deep with this, so they can get to a good place and be the best version of themselves, so they can parent at their best.'

This is you. Whether you became a mother through a test tube or a one-night stand or the most romantic moment of your life, you're here. And you are running as far and as deep as you can to transform. That's what you do. You're a mama.

> Grit as true strength

When I first heard the word 'grit', something switched. I realised that this is what I had been trying to understand about being strong, and that I had never quite grasped. And in my grasping for it, I had totally misunderstood and had thought that being strong meant pushing through, no matter what.

Kundalini yoga teaches that a woman's true strength comes from grit and grace. Grit is the part of you that says, 'I've got this.' Grit is what gets you out of bed when you've been up all night cleaning up vomit, and sees you still doing the washing, the cooking, the cleaning, the nurturing. It is the determination and commitment that we need to stick with something long term; to keep going even when it feels like it won't work; to show up every single time. It's the voice that says, 'Keep going, it will all work out.'

But I have discovered that many of us have lost our grit. I cried big hot tears of emotion when I first realised this. I was in a Kundalini yoga class. As my teacher was sharing the teachings of grit and grace, I silently sobbed, 'Oh, that's it. That's what I've lost. I've lost my grit.'

Over years of broken sleep and a broken thyroid, and all the other crap that modern life had thrown at me, I had become so bone-tired that the little fire inside me, that truly believes in **me**, had almost been extinguished. Almost. None of us have lost it completely—it's just been so drained by the pressure, the busyness, and that Inner Mean Mama voice telling us we're crap and we're doing it all wrong and what's the point anyway, that it's only a faint flicker. But do not doubt its existence.

Grit is what gets me up in the morning to meditate.

Grit is what drives me to keep learning about and healing all my inner stories that don't serve me.

Grit is what keeps my vision of who I want to be, and how I want to parent, live and love, alive.

But that little flame needs to be fanned. The little belief in myself that says, 'You've got this, Amy' needs to be stoked every single day.

Stop and think for a moment about a mother and all she does every day. Perhaps don't do this exercise by imagining yourself, but instead think of someone else (we always have a warped view of our own selves). Think of a heavily pregnant mother, waddling around with a baby heavy in her pelvis. Think of childbirth, and breastfeeding, and hours of rocking and shooshing. Think of a woman walking into work, game face on, trying to hide that she's only had three hours sleep. Think of a woman at the bedside of her child in hospital, quizzing the doctors on what is happening, all the while keeping light and positive, to ensure her child isn't scared. Think of a woman standing at the sink, so tired her vision is blurry, washing the dishes before the next round of meals in just a few hours.

Need some more examples of grit? You have it now.

You have grit. You may feel that the fire in you has almost extinguished too, but it hasn't. It never will. We all have it, but it's time to throw on some kindling. What's really important here is to see and accept that there is a difference between the masculine strength of fighting your way through, and the feminine, inner grit that comes from knowing who you really are.

It's the belief that you don't need to prove anything. That's the key. Can you see the difference? One is pushing through, trying to prove to everyone they can do it, that they are strong. And the other is believing in herself and doing what needs to be done, with the deep inner soundtrack of 'You're amazing!'

I would love you to imagine that small flame of perseverance, of resilience, of **grit** inside you. Find where it is in your body (usually the belly), and feel it grow stronger. Feel a connection with it. Know that this is who you really are:

You are a woman. You are a mother. You are the source and the hub and the pivot.

You do not need to **fight** anymore. You are grit and grace.

› Strength is breaking up with superwoman

Brooke McAlary is a mama who spent her first years of motherhood believing she needed to do it all. As a small business owner, wife, and soon to be mum of two, she believed she had followed the rules and was doing what she should. She had the house and the garage full of 'stuff', so surely that meant she'd made it?

It took a breakdown, including severe postnatal depression, to realise the truth about that dream. And after a slow recovery in which she questioned all her former beliefs of 'success', Brooke is now connecting with millions around the globe through her weekly podcast and bestselling books by asking: *Is this the life we really want?*

The fact is, most of us are chasing something that we think will make us happy, pretending that we're strong. But, as Brooke shares, this is not strength. 'I have always been someone who was highly anxious, highly stressed. Someone who was really focused on appearing like I had everything together. It really mattered to me that I was a person who appeared to have their life sorted. I was running my own business, our daughter was only one-and-a-bit, I was heavily pregnant, renovating our house, doing all of these things that I thought I needed to do, in order to keep up with the Joneses. My husband was working long hours in the city, so we didn't see much of him during the week.

'And then, about six weeks after our second child (our son) was born, I had a massive breakdown. Looking back, there were many signs that came before it. But one day I found myself talking out loud to my reflection in the mirror, just saying, "I hate you, I hate you, I hate you" over and over again. That was the moment that the tiny little voice in the back of my head said, "Actually, this is not how motherhood needs to be."

'Up until that point, I think I thought that feeling numb, feeling sad, feeling angry and feeling resentful were motherhood. I didn't know any different, so that's what I thought it looked like. But thankfully, on that particular day, there was a little voice that said, "Actually, it doesn't need to look like this." That was the day I called my husband and said, "I'm not okay". From that point on, everything started to change, very gradually.'

Brooke spent the coming months trying to unlearn this superwoman mentality and, as she describes it, trying to 'keep up with the Joneses'.

She continues: 'It was a very slow and painful process at first! I began to see a psychiatrist, and I remember when she suggested that I should perhaps slow down and do less, I had such a reaction. I remember thinking, "Slow down? Do less? Seriously?" Doing less was for underachievers. Slowing down was for weak, boring people. No-one talks about how unhappy we are as we push our way to get the things we're told we need. At some point, you have to stop and realise that if I'm putting off my happiness to get to these points on the horizon, maybe I'm looking for my happiness in the wrong places. What I found was that you had to turn around and go back. Go back to what's important to you. Don't worry about what we're told we need to be pursuing, or what we **should** be doing.'

Asking for help, breaking up with busyness, letting go of that endless pursuit of the next thing, chasing the dream even though it might not be the dream anymore—this is real strength. And it is what matrescence is here to teach us.

In the end, Brooke's awakening came from an unusual exercise: writing her eulogy. After picking up a book of writing prompts in a bookshop one day, she randomly opened it to a suggestion that she write her own eulogy. 'Everything changed,' she says. 'Writing that helped me figure out what my personal values were, and what I wanted my family to say about me at the end of my life. But the bigger part of it was actually realising that I was not living my life according to them at all. As much as I tried to tell myself that I was, when I weighed it up against my day-to-day life, I realised just how far away I was from that.

Things didn't get easier, but it became simpler to start making decisions based on my values, and putting them at the centre.'

> ## Empowering yourself

Let me tell you a story. My sister was pregnant a few months ahead of me with my little boy. She went into her birth preparation with the zest most new mamas do—with a total dedication to having a divine natural birthing process. She and her husband are both very 'mind over matter' kinda people, and approach most things in life with the confidence that they can make them happen. They did the Calmbirth course, they read the books. Her husband viewed coaching my sister through labour as a personal challenge—there was no way they weren't going to get through it!

And then, just as the Universe (and our children) so often does, her little boy had other plans.

Her son was breech. And I mean really, really happy to be upside down, with his head close to his mama's heart. That stubborn little guy did not budge, no matter what my sister did—and boy, did she try everything! There were two attempts at turning him; there was acupuncture, yoga and herbs. I think she and her husband single-handedly pumped the Google search engine for 'how to turn a breech baby' to record numbers, but this bub wasn't going anywhere. But his parents' plans were.

This is the miracle of parenthood. My sister had gotten what she wanted most of her life. At university she was known as Teflon Woman, as nothing bad ever stuck to her. She was blessed, most would say. But this really threw her. Why couldn't she get what she wanted?

It didn't help that her sister had had a natural breech birth. My experience of a beautiful and empowering breech birth with my middle child must have felt like someone waving their award for best in class right in front of your nose, just moments after you discovered you'd failed. I was supremely aware that my experience and insights were only pouring salt on her very tender wounds, so I backed off. This was her experience, and I tried to respect that.

Finally, after many tears of anger and fear, they gave up their dream of a natural birth, and accepted their obstetrician's advice that for her and her baby, a caesarean was the only option. She could have hung onto that anger and fear. She could have stayed in the 'woe is me' camp, and I don't think I would have blamed her. It wasn't fair that she couldn't have a go at it like I did, and it wasn't fair that a C-section with her first baby would make a natural birth with her second less likely.

But do you know what my supremely capable and inspiring sister did? She totally empowered herself to make that birth the most natural version of a caesarean she could. She spent night and day researching the latest on the health of the baby after a C-section. She had a trainee midwife with her, to ensure their wishes were met. She had a meeting with the obstetrician about letting the cord blood run out until it stopped pulsing, and arranged for her husband to cut the cord. They organised to have skin-to-skin contact with her husband **and** her in recovery. I have recently heard that the midwife attending the birth said that in the two years since their son's birth, she has never seen a caesarean like it.

But wait. On the morning of the planned birth, my sister got up before dawn and filled her lounge room with candles, put on the birthing playlist she had so heart-rendingly put together for their dream natural birth, then sat on the floor and spoke to her unborn baby boy. She sat there, preparing for his arrival, bonding with the process. At one stage, her husband woke up and came down to find her there, and he joined her. They sat on that floor and had the beautiful natural bonding experience they had dreamed of.

And then, just days after they came home from hospital with their new baby, my sister ran a bath and got into it with her newborn son, and lay in the water, 'giving birth' to him in her mind. She held him against her wet skin, and just lay there with him. Feeling him become a part of her.

You can't tell me that that is not one of the most empowering and beautiful birthing stories you have ever heard. And you can't tell me that my sister's approach to what could have been one of the biggest disappointments in her life was not one of true strength and resilience.

Strength is always a choice to pick yourself up and find a better way. Strength is knowing that there are going to be challenges, and tough nights, and moments when you just want to scream (and maybe you will). But you get through it. You learn from it. You grow, you find your power again, and you keep on going.

You have that. We all do. And if you can't see the power in your birth, or your time as a new mama, or even now, then it's time to rewrite the story. It's time to talk to yourself as you would to your very best friend, and point out all the amazing times you **didn't** crumble under pressure, and just how resilient you are.

Let go of that comparison and judgement of what should have been 'right', and acknowledge that you did it. You did it the best way you could. As you do this, you may feel a mix of emotions: anger at how much judgement the world has placed on you; sadness at how long you have denied yourself this loving attention; grief at what was. All of this is okay—and really important.

Acknowledge what is coming up. Be angry in your journal at how much you've judged yourself. Have a beautiful big releasing cry at how harsh you've been on yourself, as you sit in a warm bath tonight!

It is not your fault. The world has taken away from us one of the most essential qualities of being a woman: the right to honour ourselves. How are we meant to feel proud of bringing life into this world and managing all the demands of a modern life, when society around us does not?

So feel all the feels—with kindness. Shower yourself in love. Know that you are releasing layers and layers of judgement and fear, and that you are safe. Nothing will come up that's not ready to.

And then create a moment for yourself to honour the rite of passage you have been through. Write down all the moments when you have found the resilience, grit and pure inner power to get through and rise up. Find those times, and hang onto them. Be proud of them. Let them define you, so that next time that Inner Mean Mama kicks in with her negative 'you can't do this' voice, you've got a sassy answer for her. 'Oh, really? Well, I got through that; so yes, I can!'

STRENGTH ACTIVITY > Accepting Your Birth

Not all of us have had a dream caesarean. Nor a great natural birth. Post-traumatic stress and grief after a difficult or 'out of our power' birth is a very real thing; it can mean we start our journey as a mother feeling completely disconnected from the actual process of becoming a mother.

In my experience, we can forgive ourselves and the people involved, and reclaim a little of that strength. It's painful and very emotional, but I have had dozens of mamas write to me after doing the following exercise to say how much it helped them heal. I've had mamas say it changed the way they felt about their children, and about their husbands, or doctors, or people who let them down. And most importantly, it finally allowed them to feel compassion towards themselves and acknowledge that, in the end, the very fact that they **are** a mother is enough.

So here it is …

If birth grief or disempowerment is something that is stopping you from feeling fully connected with yourself as a woman and a mother, please try answering these questions in the most gentle and self-loving way you can, and then follow with the meditation. It is best if you can make this a little ceremony (think of my sister's moment on the floor with her planned birthing music and candles), or at least choose a time when you can really feel into it.

Start by asking yourself these questions (journal the answers if you can):

> How do I feel about the birth? (If you have had more than one baby, it's really beneficial to do this separately for each birth.)
> Am I proud of the outcome?
> Do I feel empowered by the process? Or was my power taken away from me?
> Do I need to forgive myself or anyone else (perhaps your partner, your doctor, the hospital system) for what happened during the birth?
> Do I wish it had been different?

Once you have answered these questions, and spent some time thinking and reflecting on your feelings surrounding the birth, you can start the healing process.

> MEDITATION <

Close your eyes and start focusing on your breath.
Begin to notice the breath moving in and out of your
nostrils. Feel it filtering down through your body. Just
spend a few minutes really connecting with your breath.

In your mind's eye, take yourself back to the birth of your baby.
Take yourself into that room.
Feel it. See it. Smell it. Remember it. Remember how it felt.
See your face in your mind's eye—what does it look like?
How is that woman feeling right now? Is there fear
in her eyes, or is there a power and wonder? Can you
sense in your body now how it felt back then?

Go to that woman in your mind, and hold her hand.
Look deep into her eyes and tell her she is doing an amazing job.
Breathe with her. Tell her again. And again.
Surround her with love and energy.
See the power and energy of Mother Earth around her,
and all the mothers that have ever given birth before
her. She has all of that energy to call on now.
Wrap it around her.

Then, see your baby being born. Relive that moment.
The welcoming of their little spirit into
this world. That first breath.

If fear or judgement comes up, just smile at yourself
in your mind's eye again, tell yourself you did the
best you could, and send yourself love.
Tell the woman you see how amazing she is again.

Feel your baby on your chest now. Feel their skin
on your skin. See their spirit connecting with yours,
just like it did when they were inside you.
You did it. You did it. You did it. You are
a mother. You are amazing.

Your child is here, in this world, because of you.
Feel that tingling in your body? That is your power.
That is your strength. That is yours forever now.
No-one and nothing can take that from you.

Open your eyes when you are ready.

CHAPTER 6

FOCUS THREE > VALUE

Don't you get it? Can't you see? As we change our

minds, we will change the world.

And until we do, we will remain where we are.

— MARIANNE WILLIAMSON

How do we value something that is so undervalued by the world? How do we feel deeply connected and proud about that which the world glosses over—in fact, dismisses? This is our greatest challenge, mamas.

We were told—either unconsciously or straight to our face—that being 'just a mum' was a waste of our talent and skills. What else are you going to do in this world? You can be and have anything you want! That was the catchcry of our generation. And while it has taken women into roles and positions around the world that our grandmothers would never have dreamed of, it has also completely disconnected us to the very important work of being a mother.

As Dr Catherine Birndorf from The Motherhood Centre of New York told me: 'So much of the struggle with this has to do with valuing the experience of a woman—of being female in this world at this time. I just think if this was happening to a man, it would be well known; it would have been studied and researched properly. There are so many ways that women have been put aside—including the way we haven't valued the experience of being a mother. It makes me very sad to say that, but I do think it's true.'

Let's go back, again, to look at why it is we so undervalue our role as mother. I do so because at the very core of it all, what I want you to feel and reflect on is this: **Your value is so much more than the world tells you it is.**

So, let's go back and look again, because it wasn't always this way.

Long ago, the goddess was the ultimate source of wisdom and power. She was celebrated for her intuition and her insight. She was consulted, revered, celebrated. As Judith Duerk says in *Circle of Stones*: 'It was for her insight and authority in things unseen that woman was most valued.' In other words, it was her deep knowing, feeling and wisdom that was most honoured.

How things have changed! Intuition is dismissed as 'woo-woo mumbo jumbo'. Our instincts are dismissed by doctors and scholars and experts. And over time, our trust in ourselves and that little whisper inside are eroded. Instead, we're dismissed and told that our true worth comes from our value to the economy:

how much we earn, what we contribute, how far we have come, how quickly we meet our targets.

For years, I have coached and supported mamas in this process of reclaiming who they are, and this particular point is always the hardest. Undoing and unlearning the deep belief system that their value comes from productivity is hard. Revealing to them that their real worth comes from their inner knowing, their ability to heal and be healed, their inner grit, and their deep believing is even harder. Of course it is, when our very education system is built on a foundation of comparison and competition.

But again, mama, I invite you to crack open a little here.

Your value does not come from what you thought it did. And it cannot be measured by anyone outside of you. Your value is yours alone to decide. So let's make a decision to honour the unseen. Once again, this is the gift of matrescence.

> Valuing motherhood

My mother used to say to my sister and me that the greatest thing she'd ever done in her life was to have us. That used to shock me. Be a mum? That's it? But what about travel, your career, great moments with friends, Dad!? Now, having been blessed with three of my own, I feel exactly the same. This is the best thing I will ever do.

There will be others who will make a greater contribution to the world than I. Other writers will reach more mums, other businesswomen will have more success. There will be other friends who will be there for my friends, and my husband will have other joys in his life as well as me. But there will only ever be one mother to my children. They may explore the world and live thousands of miles away from me, but I will always be 'home' to them. Me. Just me. They will walk into my home, or hear my voice on the phone, and I will be able to comfort them and inspire them like no other. And that is the greatest role in the world.

But it took me many, many years to acknowledge this. And even more to deeply believe it to be true.

I was going to be a foreign correspondent. After living in Japan for two years—including a year studying International Politics at a university in Tokyo—my path was set. I signed up to the ABC straight after my honours degree at university, and worked my way up from producer of the *Morning Show* in the backwaters of regional South Australia to Sydney. With that came a whole lot of prestige. Sure, it wasn't yet Tokyo, but I was on my way. I had a plan. Did that plan involve three little ones running around me? Hell no! I was pretty certain my day-to-day life would look more like *The Newsroom* than *Bad Moms*.

So often, the dream we had in our twenties does not live up to our expectations. Influenced by images of four single and fantastic gals in New York City, we pictured our lives filled with cocktails, promotions and power games. Happiness and satisfaction would come from being more—more skinny, more rich, more successful. We were going to rule the world!

But then there was the ticking biological clock. Not since World War II have we been having so many babies—and I know why. After years of putting our eggs on hold, we've heeded the warning not to leave it too late, and we're having babies in droves. Mostly with a secret hope that we can still be that sassy, sexy, successful woman we pictured all those years ago. And now we all know how that turned out.

So here's the thing: we can't sit around waiting for society to start valuing our roles as mothers more. We can't expect our workplace to start honouring mothers, our government to change its view on stay-at-home mums, or our judgemental neighbours to evolve past their bigoted view of where our place is in the world. We have to start with ourselves. And each other.

Until we start valuing ourselves as women, mothers, wives and partners, we will always feel torn. We will always be reaching for 'more' validation, because we don't have it inside ourselves. Like I've said so many times, unless we do it for ourselves, we will never find it.

But how? I believe we do it in two ways: we redefine success now we are a mother and what that really looks like; and we start to take action in our everyday lives to value who we are and what we are doing.

> Redefining success

There's something about the images we create in our minds as teenagers that are very powerful. Full of hope and hormones, we construct this image of who we are going to be when we grow up … and build her into a goddess. She is everything we long to be, whether we can see clearly what she does and how she does it, or whether it's just a general 'feeling' of what we're going to become. It's the dream.

The problem is, that teenage girl didn't have a clue what she was talking about. She didn't know about mortgages or mama-hood, she didn't know about endless emails or empty ambition. She thought that high heels, a cool boyfriend, and an exciting job was where it's at, and so she created a masterpiece with that in mind. And we've been hanging on to her ever since.

Even after all the work I've done on my superwoman ego, I still struggle with this at times. There's part of me that still wonders if I sold out, or let go of my dream too quickly. I feel like I've let myself down, because I didn't do what I thought I would do, and I'm not where I thought I would be. There are times when I see a foreign correspondent on the news and feel pangs of jealousy. Was that meant to be me?

I've put part of my dream on hold, even though I thought I never would.

The truth is, I want to be there for my family. Being a mama and wife is part of my daily 'job' at the moment—and it's taken me a while to be okay to say that out loud.

This has been big. It's brought up a truckload of issues surrounding women's rights to work, my own (outdated) beliefs, what's politically correct, and judgement. A whole lot of judgement. Why can't I have it all? What about my own dreams? Maybe, if I juggle enough, move things around enough, book in some more day care and hire an after-school nanny, I can still get it all?

I tried. I really did try. And I failed, miserably. What I came to realise was that all I was doing was trying to prove myself to everyone. I was hanging onto that image I'd set two decades earlier and was blindly chasing it, even if it wasn't what I wanted anymore.

So ... what does this mean for that woman I've been idolising for thirty years?

The Feminine Mystique is a book written by Betty Friedan in the early 1960s, widely credited with sparking the beginning of second-wave feminism in the United States. It affected me deeply. She described the pain so many women felt, being stuck as a housewife in the 1950s. But it was the recognition of their struggle and deep despair at the daily reality of just being someone's wife and mother that affected my own story.

We can no longer ignore that voice within women that says: 'I want something more than my husband and my children and my home'.

I was brought up with that story. That belief is in my DNA— and I'm guessing it's in yours. Our mothers were the children of those mothers, and they saw firsthand how unhappy a controlled, 'caged in' (as Betty Friedan described it) woman at home was. They saw the pain their mothers went through, not being able to venture into their own dreams or ambitions. They witnessed their mothers give all of themselves to their families, and decided that they wanted more.

And their mothers wanted that too. The deep stirring that began in the late 1950s, around women being chained to the sink, saw mothers whisper dreams of something different into their daughter's ears. *Take on the world; be more than someone's mum and wife.* And so our mothers did. They came out into the world determined to right the wrongs of that time. And in the process, they gave birth to us with the same deep-seated desire to **do more.**

Can you understand how this was planted deep into our psyche too? Is there any wonder we struggle with the transition to motherhood, when so much of what we carry within is full of judgement about this role?

If we are to look at matrescence as a natural and beautiful opportunity to emerge anew, then what we most need to do, to make it as painless as possible, is to recognise this: **It is our attachment to our beliefs about the role of mother and wife and woman that causes us the most pain.**

It is how we value what we are doing, and who we are in the eyes of the world, that causes us to suffer so much. Can you see that?

Let's take the role of mother. What did being a mum mean to you before you started on your mothering experience? How did you feel about your mum, and the job she did? How do you feel about her life, and her happiness? Do you want to do things the same, or differently? And what did your mother teach you about womanhood and motherhood? What did she whisper in your ear?

I coached a mama once who was one of four daughters, raised by a full-time working mother and father. Her mother had a phenomenally successful career in a very male-dominated industry, while raising her four girls. From the day they were born, she'd taught her daughters that they could and should do anything. And that motherhood was something you could do on the side, while you chased that ambition. The problem was that my client was now a mama of a baby and a toddler trying to juggle her career, and she hated it. She didn't want to work so much anymore. She actually wanted to quit her job and stay at home. But she carried such judgement around being a stay-at-home mum that she didn't dare. For her, the balance of work and family wasn't working, but she felt paralysed about changing it.

No-one else can decide your personal balance of motherhood, relationship, passion and purpose—no-one but you. Your balance of how much you work and how much you stay at home will be uniquely yours. It has to be. If it's not, then you're living your life by someone else's definition again.

But first, you have to value what you're doing, right now. You have to find a way to free yourself from the judgement of the world around you and (yes, perhaps) the women before you, and see what you're doing in a new light. Because it is the only way to be.

> Break up with proving yourself

When we feel undervalued, we tend to start overcompensating by doing **more**. We go above and beyond to prove that we are important, that what we do matters, that **we** matter. We say 'yes' to more than we should, and load ourselves up with extra tasks, because somewhere deep inside we feel like we need to prove ourselves—again.

Saying 'yes' to everything and being everything to everyone actually undervalues how important we are.

It's so common. Especially for women. We take on extra work at our jobs, because we're worried that we're not taken seriously when working part-time. We take on extra roles at school, day care and kindy, because we feel like we should be doing more while we're 'just at home'. We even take on extra roles within our family, because we believe we need to. Can you see a pattern here?

We're trying to prove we're enough. Again, we're ignoring the transformative power of matrescence to redefine every part of ourselves—our worth, our value, our productivity, our purpose. We slip right back into the old thinking again. We burn ourselves out, proving we're still who we used to be.

Accepting a new value system is tough. When I slowed down and looked at mine for what it really was, I realised that my dreams had changed. My idea of success had transformed along with my true self, and it was time to let go of that old ideal of what I wanted my life to look like. I didn't want to be the stressed-out, multi-juggling woman I used to be, and that I used to idolise. I wanted to be free. It was time to say goodbye.

Goodbye, superwoman. I acknowledge that you have been with me since I was a little girl, when I believed that you were a goddess. I have had images of you on my vision board for decades, and have judged every decision in my life by whether you would do it too. I love you, because you have played a very important part in my life until now, but I don't want to be you anymore. I have changed, and while it's still terrifying at times to not have you in my mind's eye as my goal, I am ready to let you go.

I know a new woman now. She's the one I am becoming. And I'm really okay with that now. I'm not going to just say 'yes' to things out of fear of not doing enough anymore.

What about you? Look at what you do and who you are with new eyes. Ask yourself: is it time to rewrite this story?

This is your invitation to return to your true value—the woman rising, the goddess, the creator, the centre of it all. This is your invitation to walk with me, and thousands upon thousands of women around the world who are remembering who they really are. Remembering, and owning.

Start by valuing yourself without judgement. When you do, you will no longer have any tolerance for the hustle. You will no longer say 'yes' when you really want to say 'no'. You will be free from the endless pursuit of proving yourself. You will value all you do.

> Redefine your money story

Matrescence is an opportunity to clear out the old beliefs—whether your own or those of society—and write new ones. And our relationship with money and worth is yet another area of our life that is open to a new narrative. However, nothing brings up more fear and judgement than money, especially when it comes to a massive change in how much you earn.

This has been a big issue in my marriage and my life. When I met my future husband, I was making twice as much as he was, and was definitely the go-getter in our relationship. So when things changed dramatically as I stepped back from my career, my sense of identity changed dramatically too, over and over again as each new baby arrived.

Kate Northrup is a mama, entrepreneur and bestselling author of *Money, a Love Story*. Having found herself deep in debt and with a toxic relationship with money before mamahood, she began to explore her feelings around money, abundance and debt, and how to change her story to one of love. Since then, she has been deeply committed to showing women (and men) around the world how to achieve real financial freedom. Since becoming a mama, this has taken on even more purpose.

How do we change our money story as part of matrescence? Kate says, 'We live in a difficult time for women when it comes to money. Our whole identity has been attached to the idea of wealth and success and grow, grow, grow, climb, climb, climb. It's about the hustle. And then we have so many romantic ideas of how this might work. Before my first daughter came along, I had this idea that I could sidestep the pull between motherhood and work. And I thought that if I could create financial wellbeing and an income, whether I was working or not, I wouldn't have that same tension. And the truth is—I was not able to avoid it! I still went through the same deep questioning of who I was and how I was going to be successful as a woman and a mother.

'Mothers need a place that honours the very unique experience of being a mother. You really need to be able to give yourself more space. I see mom entrepreneurs trying to operate as though they don't have children, and for what? Obviously, they need to put food on the table and pay the bills, I get that. But then beyond that, there's a lot of extra pressure we create for ourselves, when we get whipped up into a froth about "keeping up".'

When so much of our sense of self is deeply tied to our busyness and our worth in the workplace, we totally undervalue what we're actually doing during these years: raising our children, and becoming anew. Whether we work or not, the truth is we won't be able to do what we used to do—not for a while. So again, it's time to redefine.

'Whether you work for yourself, for someone else, or have decided not to work at all, having kids is a really great opportunity to divorce our worth from dollars,' says Kate. 'If we stay tied to the belief that our value is tied to how much we earn in an hour, we will always struggle. We really need to learn how to break this pattern of connection between time and money. Becoming a parent is so critical, because parenting is not valued in our society—raising children is not valued in our society. So if you look at your day and see you changed six diapers, did ten loads of laundry, read five books, and played for an hour on the floor—none of that makes money, but it's valuable.

'Disconnecting our worth from our income is a discipline we have to practise though. Especially if you are not back at work and don't plan to be, and your partner is bringing in the income—your self-worth will be eroded. But it doesn't have to be. Just because society doesn't celebrate child rearing, that doesn't mean we can't celebrate child rearing in our own homes. It has to start with us. Women will say, "How can I get my husband or boss to value what I do more?" and it always has to start with us. Because when we value ourselves and hold ourselves in high regard, the world rearranges itself around us to reflect that.'

> ## Become the new you

Our value is more than just what we do each day—it's also how we feel about ourselves. And we need to feel good about ourselves, mamas. For a long time, I found this part of the journey difficult to marry with the spiritual focus I was so passionate about. I wanted women to embrace self-enquiry and honour the deep stirring within them, but I also knew that, for me, how I looked, how I dressed, and how I felt about myself mattered.

If we don't value who we are, thinking, 'Oh, what's the point anyway, no-one is going to see me today', then we begin to give up on ourselves. We see this all around us: a woman loses herself and any appreciation for who she is, then she starts to not care what she looks like, or what she feeds herself. She can't be bothered exercising, and she just throws 'any old thing' on every day. It's all about intention though—if you're intention is to hide, to not bring any attention to yourself, to wait until the baby is older or you feel better about your belly, then you will never emerge with confidence.

This has been a tough part of this journey to share. The very first time I wrote a blog about the importance of putting on something that makes you feel good every day, I received an absolutely heartbreaking email from a reader. 'How dare you make mummies feel the pressure to be beautiful on top of everything else they have to do each day!', she screamed at me. There were days when she could only just manage to put her tracksuit pants on, and it was not my place to make her feel bad about that!

I was devastated that I had made a mama feel that way, so I retreated from this topic for a very long time.

But you know what? I stand by that blog now. I've spent a lot of time since then talking about this, reflecting on it, and working through it. I now know in my heart of hearts that how we feel about ourselves is reflected in how we present ourselves. And if we are to fully love, accept and celebrate ourselves as women again, then we need to feel good, for God's sake!

I actually don't care if it's your tracksuit pants that make you feel divine, or if it's your oldest skirt that has a few baby stains on it. Once again, this is about how you **feel**.

Think about it—before babies, we used to get dressed every day to present ourselves to the world. We had our work clothes, our social clothes, our 'looks'. It was part of our identity. And yes, a true spiritual yogi does not concern herself with what she looks like; but I'm assuming you're still on my level of awakening and are not ready to live without some beautiful things in your life.

So here's my thought: **it all starts with mascara**. This one little act can become the catalyst for a whole transformation in how you feel about yourself. If you focus on it in the morning, rather than just mindlessly getting ready and rushing out the door, you've started a connection with yourself. This one little act doesn't only hide the tired eyes and all the wrinkles, it also says to the Universe, 'Yes, I'm showing up today! I'm shattered, I haven't shaved my legs since last summer, but I'm here. I'm doing my best. And I'm worth it.'

This is how we start to rebuild the whole. We bring those split parts of ourselves back again with the small daily actions of mascara, or a nice bra, or choosing an essential oil to honour our mood. It's not for anyone else but you—the woman underneath all that mama exterior.

In her book, *Simple Abundance: A Daybook of Comfort and Joy*, Sarah Ban Breathnach says, 'As you become more intimate with your authentic self—as you recover your true, incandescent identity—there will come a gradual but undeniable physical transformation. It is absolutely impossible to commit to your spiritual growth, to awaken your own radiant Light, and not have it reveal itself on the outside.'

Allow yourself to explore who you are now through what makes you feel good, and give yourself permission to be a woman again. Show yourself that you are important and valued, by giving yourself the time and energy to check in each morning and ask, 'What is it I feel like today?'

VALUE ACTIVITY > Wardrobe Clean Out

This is meant to be fun. This is meant to be a reflection of your transformation—shedding the old you, the parts of you that you've been hanging onto 'just in case'. No more putting yourself on hold, and waiting for the body/job/baby to change.

If you don't love it, donate it. If it doesn't suit who you are anymore (you know that tight, tight skirt that you loved ten years ago?) then pass it on. If you don't feel your best in it, move it on.

We have an obsession in our society with having a big wardrobe—even if it means collecting clothes that aren't right for us anymore. But all that achieves is a sense of overwhelm in the mornings, and a sense that we 'have all these clothes and nothing to wear'.

If it's not who you are anymore, let it go. Make room for the best. Clear out the clutter. Bring in a little Marie Kondo, and ask yourself, 'Does this bring me joy?' If the answer is 'no', then thank it for its part in your life.

Ask yourself: *Who am I now? What makes me feel confident, happy, and proud?* You deserve to feel that every single day.

And while you're at it, clean out your bathroom cabinet, make-up bag and underwear drawer. Old hair products that you never use. Clumpy mascara and blue eyeliner. Maternity bras and knickers with the elastic gone. Why do we hang onto these things??

This is not about buying lots of new things, or spending lots of money on material things. It's actually about simple abundance. Being super clear on what we need in our lives, being mindful when we reach into our bathroom cabinet in the morning, treating our morning routine like the beautiful ritual it should be, and telling the Universe we only want the best.

CHAPTER 7

FOCUS FOUR > GRACE

You can approach life with both fierceness and grace.

— BRENÉ BROWN

Motherhood has been my awakening. That is certain. And I believe this is the gift of matrescence for us all.

When you consider the definition of 'awakening' in any of the spiritual texts, yogic teachings or religious philosophies, there is a common theme. In summary. an awakening is when the confused and frightened self transcends to a higher consciousness, to an awareness full of love and peace. It's a shift in consciousness, a realisation of something that was previously unseen or unknown. With that in mind, matrescence is most certainly an awakening. And one of the happy consequences of this awakening is the awareness and embodiment of grace.

For many years on my motherhood journey, I felt there was something missing. I got the self-kindness; I'd realised the truth of my strength; I'd even begun to value myself differently. But there was still something missing.

At first, I thought it was a softening, a more feminine way of approaching life. When I looked at the way I'd been living my life, the driving force had been a masculine approach, so maybe it was a more feminine way of doing things that I was missing? But 'switching on' the feminine still came from my head—not my heart. It still didn't allow me to honour this new awakening within.

Marianne Williamson describes 'everyday grace' as 'having hope, finding forgiveness, and making miracles'. When I first read that, I knew I'd found the answer. The final jigsaw piece that my heart had been searching for: **grace**.

From what I've learnt, grace is all about how we act in our daily lives, how we come back to what we know to be true, and how we respect ourselves. Grace is how we handle a meltdown in the middle of the supermarket, how we put mascara on to cover our bloodshot, tired eyes, and how we choose to nourish our bodies each day.

Grace is how we show up in this life, every single day. Grace is a choice. And when the shit hits the fan, it's about surrendering to it, and accepting it for what it is.

Surrender—oh, how we modern-day mamas ignore that key element to happiness. We hang onto our goals and our plans and our set-in-concrete ideals of what life is meant to look like, and God help us when it doesn't live up to that image.

Perhaps this clinging to our ideals is a big part of our disconnection? I know that in my own journey, letting go of all my previous ideas of a happy life has been a big element in my healing. But let me clarify that. It's not just any old letting go, because I do think we overuse that phrase. *Just let it go.* 'Oh, thank you for reminding me of that simple idea,' she says, while internally screaming, 'I can't just let it go!'

So here's where it changed for me: **letting go is opening up to other possibilities**.

A very wise woman once described it to me like this …

Most of us go through life with our fists tightly clenched around what we want—so tightly it aches. It's like we're hanging on for dear life. But when we understand surrender, and 'let it all go', our hands open, our palms open up, our fingers uncurl, and we are open to whatever comes.

I loved that. Whenever I think about that analogy, my hands physically soften. I start to let go.

Elizabeth Gilbert sums it up perfectly too, when she talks about accepting what is. She encourages us to 'move on swiftly, with humility and grace. Don't fall into a funk about the one that got away. Don't beat yourself up. Don't rage at the gods above. All that is nothing but distraction, and the last thing you need is more distraction.'

Motherhood is calling us not to distract ourselves from ourselves anymore. It's begging us to get real about what we really want, and undo all those ancient beliefs we are carrying.

This is also about perfectionism. The deeper I go into the spiritual awakening of women as mothers, the more I truly feel that at the very core of it, it is our grip on perfectionism, control, being on top of everything and having it turn out like we envisioned, that is at the centre of our unhappiness.

It wasn't meant to be like this. We had an image in our minds of a beautiful, serene baby, and long catch-ups on perfectly clean picnic rugs in the park with our equally serene mothers' group. That's what we equated grace with: a mixture of some sort of Holy Mother and Audrey Hepburn. How wrong we've been.

Grace is keeping the faith—faith that this is exactly where we are meant to be, and exactly what we are meant to be learning. Faith that this too will pass.

Has there ever been a more powerful mantra for a stressed-out new mama than: *This too shall pass?* Oh, how often that has got me through. And after three babies, I know this for sure: everything does pass, and I will always get through. I have trust in myself and the law of the Universe now, and I have belief in my own strength. I'll get through whatever it is, because I always do. As will you.

As Anne Lamott says in *Plan B: Further Thoughts on Faith,* 'Faith includes noticing the mess, the emptiness and discomfort, and letting it be there until some light returns.' We need that faith, mama. When it really is all mess and emptiness and discomfort, we really do need that level of faith and grace to know we'll be okay.

So how do we do that when we really, really don't want what's happening right now? How do we keep the faith, and surrender to what is, when it's all crap?

We have to work on it, every single day. In my darkest times, when my heart was broken and I doubted any good would come of it, I had to physically act every day to connect to my belief that it was going to be okay. I had to get out of my head and that constant replaying of what had gone wrong, and stop myself from fretting over the future, and just get into what I know for sure. What I know is true.

It often looked like this: 'I know I can survive this, because I survived (insert amazing time in my past which I now marvel I got through). I let go of control of this, and get out of the way with my planning, worrying and stressing. I surrender to what is.'

Control is rooted in fear. But we have now discovered that with kindness, a true understanding of strength and a redefined worthiness of ourselves, we can now recognise that fear is just the plain old Inner Mean Mama pattern and surrender.

A Course In Miracles is a 1976 book by Helen Schucman, who tells us, 'If you knew who walked beside you on this path you have chosen, fear would be impossible.' In other words, if we knew that there was a bigger plan, a force so much greater than us that was walking right beside us, we'd soften. We'd let go.

Please know that whatever your belief system is around what that force is, it's there. You can let go a little.

> Grace is presence

Here's a breakthrough thought that blew my mind when I first saw it for what it was: **multi-tasking doesn't work**. In fact, multi-tasking is the source of most of my meltdowns, most of my tears, and most of my shameful mama moments.

Whenever I've snapped at the kids for asking me the same question over and over again, I've usually been thinking about seven different things at once. The times I have burst into tears or thought, 'I just can't do this anymore', or reached for a wine while cooking dinner, have usually been when I've been trying to send an email on my phone, while chopping onions, and breaking up a sibling fight over who gets to use the pink pen first.

I haven't been present in the moment. I haven't been focused on the task at hand. And I haven't been in touch with my thoughts. At all. And so what happens? I lose it.

Multi-tasking does not work. That cliché we were all told as young girls has seriously backfired and caused us all to think that juggling a business with babies and a bolognaise on the stove is next to godliness. But it ain't. It's the cause of our stress, and is at the heart of our dislike of who we are as women and mothers.

You are not nailing it, if you're so frazzled you can't breathe. You're not winning at life, if you're juggling your email inbox while juggling a baby on your hip. Don't breastfeed while typing. Please.

Again, this is a lie we've been fed to keep us productive. Once again, it's dismissing the feminine energy of motherhood, and not allowing us to just surrender into the moment. Be here now, one thing at a time. This has changed how I react—to everything.

Next time you reach for your phone to check social media while pushing your little one on the swing, take a moment and repeat this mantra: *Only this in this moment.*

So often I've found myself reaching for my phone while breast-feeding my baby. This was one of the most sacred and beautiful opportunities for me to connect with my spirit, and be in the moment, but I would be mindlessly scrolling through my feed, peering into other people's lives. My baby would be sucking, with her or his hand playing with my hair or wrapped around my little finger, and I would be somewhere else.

Other times, when reading my girls their bedtime story, I would get to the end and not remember a single word. Isn't it amazing that our brains can multi-task like that? We can read a story out loud, with animated voices and all, but our minds are going over the fight we had with our husband that morning.

Both of these examples could have been perfect occasions to practise mindfulness. To be 100 per cent in the moment. Our children provide a million opportunities a day for us to surrender and just 'be'; but we are so trained to multi-task that slowing our mind down and focusing on their little words or their inquisitive faces is totally foreign.

A child psychologist once told me that children often share their most intimate thoughts just before bed. There is something about being tucked up, ready for sleep, that opens them up to sharing what **really** happened at school that day. This has happened so many times with my girls. Right before lights out, one of them will suddenly ask me what happens when you die, or admit that they are being bullied at school. Of course, my first reaction is usually, 'Really? Right now? But it's already half an hour past your bedtime, the kitchen is a mess, and I've got seven emails to send tonight!' But ever since I've started to try and slow down, be in the moment, and be open to more grace in my life, I've breathed past those initial reactions, and centred back in on their little faces.

I don't want to miss this. I don't want to rush through their sharing with me, because of what the clock says. I don't want to miss that little hand on my breast as I feed them to sleep. Whatever it is … I want to be fully present for it. I want to be out of my head, and **here**.

This is grace. But it's not perfection. It's clarity, surrender, presence. It is living consciously and taking action.

Soften your tight grip on control. Instead of flying unconsciously into reaction, take a moment to notice what's really happening (as opposed to what your Inner Mean Mama is telling you is happening), and realise you have a choice. You always have a choice.

> Your healing is your greatest gift to your children
Mama, teacher and author, Elena Brower, has been teaching yoga since 1998. Her groundbreaking first book, *Art of Attention*, has

been translated into six languages. Her second book, *Practice You*, is now a bestseller and is being incorporated into teaching curricula worldwide for all ages. As she described it to me, she is here 'to make sure many millions of families get closer to nature, through their practices, through meditation, through yoga and through essential oils.' When I think of grace, it is often her evolution and presence that comes to mind.

Elena isn't perfect. She's overcome an addiction to marijuana and transformed her relationship with her mother. She has risen above her fear of money to create true wealth and freedom, and as she told me, she has become the mother she wanted to be.

'Motherhood has taught me that I am capable of change,' she told me. 'It has shown me that I'm here to evolve my own upbringing in my own way, without blame. I'm here to be creative and learn more about how to be a responsive and efficient mother, rather than reactive and hasty and nervous, which is what I was for a long time.'

'Early on in my son's life, I could see the chasm between who I was as a teacher and student of yoga, and who I was as a parent. I've spent the last decade or so learning how to be consistently steady, reliable, soft, compassionate, and open to listening in both contexts.

'Learning how to be honest and face my own struggles and patterns was something I desperately needed at one time in my life, and it has helped me be honest with myself, with my family, and with the people around me. It's helped me move out of this denial of my own goodness and this mistreatment of myself, and of sabotaging myself constantly—into a place where I believe in myself. I trust myself now. I know what I say is the truth and what I say I will do, I will do. And that is a very precious commodity.

'The three best things you can do for your kid is to show them love, respect and harmony. Live those three things, and you're good. But if you're missing any of them, you'll have children who disrespect their parents and relationships that disintegrate. It's that important.

'When I say **love**, I mean connection: sitting down to meals, daily affection, respecting bedtimes and using all that to connect. It's about talking times together, when nothing else is in the space. It's gratitude, it's kindness.

'When you have **respect**, you have dignity; you have a softer tone of voice, you're not holding a phone while talking, you're fully listening and present. You have confidence and kindness. You respect boundaries and you have a child who is capable of being able to sit in quiet spaces without needing to be distracted. I can't emphasise how important this is—children need to be capable of being bored, because that's when they find their creativity.

'And **harmony** is about the tone of your voice, the dialogue, the boundaries you uphold. I used to freaking rage at my kid—having grown up in a volatile environment where anger and emotion were shown through slamming doors and yelling louder than others, I used to rage at him. I have always had a short fuse, both internally and externally, and always battled myself because of it. But now I've learnt how to modulate my voice, so I'm not this insane contradiction of yelling one minute and then calm yogi the next. Of course, when I'm angry he knows about it, but it's not insane anymore. It's respectful.

'If you can have those three things, you are not only helping your child to be successful, but you are living with integrity. You're being responsible for your own life.'

We are not just doing this for ourselves—we are doing this for them. Through them, we learn. But for them, we grow. That is the purpose of all your struggles and pain and addictions and stories that are now coming up to be healed, mama. It is what you will pass onto them. By doing so, you'll show them how to heal themselves.

'It so important to remember that you're not perfect and you don't need to be perfect. But keep talking about your effort to be a great mama,' Elena explained so beautifully to me. 'Talk about your struggle in a way that will serve them in real life when they're older. Be honest about your relationship to your own parents; don't pretend it's great and lie about it. Tell them what's really up and stay in clear communication. Let them help you, and then they'll let you help them.'

> ## Grace is knowing who you are

I remember first connecting with Alison. Every time we'd get together on a coaching call and she'd turn the video on, I would see her sitting on the floor of her lounge room, even though the couch was right behind her. Dressed in dark colours, and sitting in darkness, she was so broken by motherhood and the loss of herself. She had just given birth to her second child, and she was overcome with judgement. She was a maternal health nurse, so her judgement came from more than just the usual new mama comparisons that many of us feel. Supporting women through early motherhood was her job. And yet here she was, on the floor, broken by motherhood.

She had lost all faith in herself. She felt like a fraud and a failure. She knew the science of what happens to a woman after birth, but it wasn't connecting. Something was missing. She knew about post-natal depression, hormonal change, social isolation and all of the medical facts about what she was experiencing, but nothing was changing.

At the time, we simply walked through how lost she felt. As always, I was the space holder, as she moved through the grief at her loss of identity and the deep shame she felt about not doing 'better'. Eventually, we started to talk about the key teachings in this book: the realisation that this is so much more than a medical and hormonal change she has gone through—it is a shedding of the old and a cracking open. I guided her to redefine herself, and reprioritise herself. I walked with her as she began her journey to finding herself again. Her new self.

Four years later, I saw a booking in my calendar for a call with a mama about my new training program. I didn't recognise the name—it had been years since we'd connected and I'd supported thousands of mamas since then. And to be totally honest, when we first started talking over video, I still didn't know who she was.

This woman was glowing. She had the most spectacular coloured scarf around her neck, huge bright earrings on, and the most gorgeous flattering haircut. She oozed feminine energy and certainty of who she was. I did not recognise her at all.

A few minutes into the call, she started to refer to a time when she was really struggling with new motherhood, and how we'd connected way back then. Suddenly, it clicked. Oh my goodness—it's Alison! The Alison who was deep in shame, sitting in the darkness, wearing dark colours, hiding from herself.

I couldn't help but cry. Here was the most divine representation of the grace and beauty of matrescence.

After I stopped gushing about her transformation, I asked her what had been the key. Looking back, what were the biggest lessons and realisations that had supported her to this new self. Her answer was so profound, I asked if I could include it here:

> 'For me, this has been a process of deep healing of perfectionism and my "not enough-ness". It's been a real soul-searching experience of discovering and embracing all of myself—my flaws and my dark side—and realising we all have a dark side. For a long time, I felt ashamed about that. I was deep in shame, and I had to learn to love myself. That was the turning point for me—delving into self-compassion, kindness, and self-love. That was what got me out of the dark

hole. I had to learn to stop myself in those moments and learn to say, "It's okay, I love you, you are good enough." And I had to practise it a thousand times a day for four years, until it became not just something I was telling myself, but something I believed.'

Practise it a thousand times a day until you believe it, mama.

GRACE ACTIVITY > Connect with Something Bigger

In the middle of the night, when I am rocking and shushing and patting the baby for the third hour, or another child has tapped me on the shoulder telling of a bad dream, grace often escapes me. While I might still outwardly be calm for my child's sake, internally I am in a world of angst. I'm planning how I'm going to teach my child so he finally sleeps on his own, or I'm running the next day's activities over and over in my head, envisioning how exhausted and horrible we're all going to feel. Or I'm just repeating my tried and tested default mantra: *I can't do this anymore.*

In those moments, my greatest strength has come from a connection to Mother Energy, which is what I call the collective energy of all the mamas who are awake, doing exactly the same thing as I am, at exactly the same time. And after connecting with thousands of mamas all around the world, at all stages of motherhood, I promise you—it is real. You are never, ever alone.

I start by imagining my street—and another exhausted mama struggling to calm her baby. And then another mama in the next few streets. And then more in my suburb. It's like a bird's-eye view over my area—hovering over it and seeing into homes where women are doing their absolute best, in the moment, to be the best mothers they can be.

Then, I hover higher ... over my city. My state. My country. And suddenly, I can see in my mind's eye thousands of women all bonded together in mothering, all shooshing and patting and trying their best. All in this together. And I breathe in that energy—that Mother Energy—and the strength of all those women, and I am stronger again. I feel proud to be part of this tribe of strength, and I know I can get through it.

When you feel you can't do this anymore, connect with Mother Energy. Connect with the truth that we are all in this, walking this path, shedding and becoming together. And if you can't find the grace or the strength from within, draw on ours. You can use ours, until you find your own again.

CHAPTER 8

FOCUS FIVE > TRUST

> To discover who she is, a woman must trust the places
> of darkness where she can meet her own deepest
> nature and give it voice ... weaving the threads of her
> life into a fabric to be named and given ... sharing it
> with the women around her, as she comes to a true
> and certain sense of herself.
>
> — JUDITH DUERK

If I'd known what matrescence was, I would have softened into the whole experience in a completely different way. If I'd known this was an awakening, a whole self-transformation, an invitation to evolve and rise, then I would have been so much kinder on myself. I would have seen my own grace; I would have forgiven myself for all the times I felt lost; I would have trusted it all.

The reason the emergence of matrescence is so profound is because it allows us to stop trying to resist what is happening, and trust it.

Just as we can surrender to the searing pain of those last contractions of childbirth, knowing that our new baby is about to emerge, so too can we trust the searing growth pains as our new self emerges. With trust, the muscles soften, the fear loosens, the body **allows.** And with trust in this process, you'll allow your divine new self to come through.

Soften, sweet mama. Trust that what is happening is all part of the plan. It's what we all go through. It's how we all rise.

When we don't trust that this is a process, we judge. Without the road map explaining that we're actually on a journey and the destination will be better than we ever imagined, we view where we are as failure. And that Inner Mean Mama emerges again. And she's fierce.

My Inner Mean Mama has a particular type of approach that has kept me captive for many, many years. Whenever I doubt myself, feel like it's all falling apart, yell, get scared—pretty much whenever I don't trust this process—she's there. And her favourite mantra is: *I can't do this anymore.*

As negative, Mean Mama, ass-kicking mantras go, it's a good one. All-encompassing, really. It can be used for work overwhelm, cleaning up vomit, arguing with my husband, or hauling my tired body out of bed after another terrible night of broken sleep. Whatever the problem, it's got it covered. It's a blanket 'I give up'. Perfection, really.

It is my default thinking whenever I am struggling.

So, do I believe her? Yes, in those moments I do. I dive right into her deceptive illusion and accept that it's all too hard. Worse than that, I believe there's no point in trying. *I can't do this anymore!* And it's just going to stay that way.

Why? Why, after all this time, is it still there? Why, after years of meditating and coaching and deep healing and self-reflection, does this voice creep up and slowly start whispering in my ear, until it grows to such a volume that I actually say the words out loud? 'I can't do this anymore!'

I know it's not because I'm weak. I know that it's not because all of the beautiful reflection and focus I've done over the years isn't working. In fact, it is only because of that work that I can recognise what that voice really is. And I know it's not because it's true. It's not; and I know that.

It keeps coming back because of what it is: my default. It's my ego. It's my shadow side that jumps in at the slightest opportunity, which is usually whenever more than one child is sick, or I've had less than six hours of broken sleep, or I've got too many things on my multi-tasking to-do list.

It keeps coming back because **that's what it does.** That's its job. That's its role in my life. That was a big realisation for me: this negative thought is there because I'm exhausted, not because I can't do it anymore.

Sometimes, it takes me a long time to acknowledge exactly what my mind is telling me. That might sound odd, but how often are you actually aware of what you're telling yourself? Do you really know what your inner voice is telling you as you go about your day, juggling a thousand things or settling an unhappy child all night? But once I hear it, and see it for what it is (fear or exhaustion), I now know exactly what to do. I know the anecdote to this fear, and it is **trust**.

Trust is the medicine you take in those moments of self-judgement.

With almost every mother I have connected with or coached, this has been a big sticking point. They just don't trust themselves anymore. Whether it's trusting enough to start nourishing themselves and stop the 3pm sugar binge; or get through a hectic morning routine without yelling; or initiate sex with their husband again. That deep belief in themselves is missing.

But here's the toughest part of my journey with this, mama. Here's the bit that has, without doubt (even more than the super-woman mentality that has dogged me my whole life) been the most painful lesson of all to learn: **I am a good person**. At my core, I am good. And with every challenge, every contraction of matrescence, every single Inner Mean Mama moment, I am unlearning and rewiring all those old beliefs that I am the complete opposite of a good person, and starting again.

This is so hard for me to believe. Raised a Catholic in the days when Catholic education started with the premise that we are all born with 'original sin', and therefore we should spend our lives trying to prove we are worthy of God's love. So I have unworthiness deep in my bones. My Mum's education was at a convent school, with nuns in habits teaching her every day. This is in my DNA. How can I trust that I am a good person, when I have spent my entire life being a 'good girl' to prove that I actually am?

In 2017, a lifetime spent proving myself came to a head when I was working my way through the metaphysical text, *A Course in Miracles*.

For many years now, I have been waking at 5am, and quietly creeping downstairs into my lounge room before any of my family wake, to sit with myself. This is truly the best way to describe it: I sit with myself. Sometimes that means meditation and journalling; sometimes it is reading a book that I am loving; sometimes it is sitting in silence, sipping my coffee and just embracing the quiet. It was and is my soul practice. It is my sanity.

For twelve months, my morning practice had included a daily email from Marianne Williamson, sharing and reading the day's message from *A Course in Miracles*. Two of my favourite gurus—the ones I've come back to over and over again over the years—swear by this text. So despite its utterly complex language, I was determined to persevere. At times I wondered why, until one sentence changed it all: *God is not vengeful.*

The relief was instant. Little did I realise how deep the belief that good things happen to good people and bad things happen to bad people had permeated my beliefs. And the deeper I dove into this belief, the more I could see its toxic energy had seeped into every part of my life.

As parents, we reward the good and punish the bad. At school, it is the same. In all areas of life, there's an underlying current of judgement that says, 'When you do good things, good things happen.' So when things got hard, or something did actually 'go wrong', my logical conclusion was that I'd done something bad.

Can you see how that totally undermines every element of trust in this process?

In my mind, whenever the kids or I yelled, or I screwed up, it was because I was in the wrong. Not once did I consider it as part of the journey. Not once did I see it as an opportunity to learn or to grow. Not once did I look at it with compassion or forgiveness. I'd done something bad. Which meant that I was bad.

Have you noticed that too? Can you see now that you may have a belief, either consciously or unconsciously, that when something bad or unwelcome comes into your world, it has something to do with you? Or that it might even be your fault?

As women, we do this. We blame ourselves for everything. As mothers, it's a particularly addictive condition. You hear mothers do this all the time. As their child is throwing themselves on the ground in a very public tantrum, you'll hear the mother saying, 'Oh, it's because I didn't give him his nap yesterday.' Or because she forgot something, or missed something, or did something. Our children's happiness is our responsibility, so if they're not happy, it's our fault. Right?

I have had mamas sob to me about the guilt they feel over discovering their child has autism or ADHD or a physical condition, believing that they are responsible in some way.

This is a burden that has been passed down to us for far too many generations; but again, acknowledging this is the gift of matrescence.

You are here to undo that belief, mama. It's up to you to realise that God/The Universe/Source/Whatever You Want To Call It is not up there somewhere keeping score. You yelled today, so I'm going to send you a parking ticket. You worked too much while you were pregnant, so I'm going to make your child sick.

Please, let's break this cycle of belief. Right here, right now!

Life is made up of deep challenges and amazing miracles in equal measure, and that is how we grow. We are not being tested because there's something wrong with us; we're being tested so we can evolve and transform into Who We Are Meant To Be. And mamahood is our greatest teacher here.

> The spiral

So how do we do this? How do we trust that the pain is simply evidence that we're growing?

About a year after Cassius' birth, I found myself back in a dark place again. The heady lightness that had come from his empowering birth experience had slowly faded, and the reality of trying to juggle my return to work at the ABC, together with my deep desire to do more with mamas around the world, was filling my head with doubt. I so wanted to leave my work in the media, knowing it wasn't for me anymore, but could I really make that work? Could I make enough money to support my family, and help enough mamas? The fear was so strong, I felt it as I breathed in each morning.

I have heard many times over that three children is the tipping point. Once you've had three, you may as well have six. Although I will not be testing out that hypothesis, bringing a third child into the mix certainly did tip us over. Add in returning to work in a highly stressful and demanding role, and I felt like all my 'good work' during the previous eighteen months—from his attempted early labour to his first birthday—was undone.

I was right back where I'd started. Had I learnt nothing? Perhaps even worse, that Inner Mean Mama voice tormented me with questions in the night: *Why am I back here again? Why does this keep happening?*

I've always struggled with this part of the process. I have always found the 'one step forwards, two steps backwards' nature of the whole self-realisation process so very difficult to accept. Of course, that's because I judged it. Again. But it was also because I never realised that the back and forth and re-emerging pattern was the whole point. It is the **whole point**.

One day, that 'why' voice in my head became too loud, and I started to feel it in every cell of my body. I felt possessed with my anger about being 'back here again'. I needed help to shift it. I needed a new perspective. So I did what all good modern mamas do and googled it. A million clicks later, I had booked an appointment for some kind of new age pattern-clearing healing, about an hour from where I lived in Sydney. Surely that would be the solution?

I have to say, the treatment itself was nothing special. I did not have any profound shifts, and at times I felt I was telling the therapist more about how energy works then she was enlightening me. The session was held in her share house out in the middle of the suburbs, all purple crushed velvet curtains and angel tarot cards everywhere. It was just not my thing.

However, as the divine Gabby Bernstein says, the Universe always has our back. Everything is always leading us to where we need to go. As I waited for her to get her massage table ready and clear the room's aura, I noticed a book on the table in front of me, *The Angels Within Us* by John Randolph Price. And of course, as I randomly opened the book, it fell open to the chapter 'The Angels of Cycles and Solutions' and to the page containing the exact answer I was seeking.

On that page was a spiral representing our energy, the process of awakening we are all here to experience:

Notice that the line of the spiral is moving up, then begins to level out and fall back, but catches itself in time and gets back on track. It then resumes its upward arc to form a new pattern and continues the coiling process in rhythmic harmony. This is what life looks like in a mystical sense, and each new 'coil' is an initiation or expansion in consciousness.

In other words, we're never really going backwards—we're just gaining momentum to go higher.

Look again at the spiral. Sometimes, it appears as if the line is going backwards. In fact, it actually is. But follow the line further and you'll see it is actually just preparing to spring up, to rise, to go higher. The backwards motion is the momentum it needs to propel up to the next level.

Any experience of contraction is the gathering of power. Could all the struggles—the 'why am I here again?'—actually be the momentum needed to break through the next layer?

Can you begin to trust this process? Can you see that life is not linear, always moving forwards in a perfectly straight line? It's a process of expansion and growth, and then a seeming backward motion, in preparation for going higher again?

Two years later I returned to this image, after another backward spiral in my life, when I was faced with the toughest parenting challenge of my life to date—severe anxiety in one of my children. Somewhere buried in my phone was the photo of that passage from the book. In the middle of the night in one of those horrible toxic moments of deep fear, I started frantically searching for it again. Once again, it allowed me to exhale, and to trust. This, too, is part of the momentum. This, too, is part of the cycle of my growth, and my daughter's.

And so that weekend, on a rare date night with my husband, I walked into a tattoo studio on King St, Newtown, in the inner-west of Sydney. I had a picture of a spiral and asked for it to be permanently drawn on my arm, so I'd never doubt again. It is my mantra and my talisman. It is my daily reminder to trust. Every single part of this birthing of me—this matrescence—has purpose. It is **all** helping me rise. Every single part of it.

Can you trust that you are emerging?

Can you believe, truly believe, that each spiral down is actually momentum to rise higher?

Can you trust matrescence, and the divine gift that is motherhood, with all its pain and joy?

Now, when times are tough, I soften into them. I smile and ask myself, 'I wonder what I'm gathering momentum for here?' I really do. I don't judge myself as being 'bad' or not worthy anymore. I don't see hardship as punishment. And amazingly, the *I can't do this anymore* mantra hardly ever shows up.

The truth is … I do want to do this, again and again. This is how I continue up the spiral. This is the purpose of life.

TRUST ACTIVITY > The Spiral of Life

One of the most important exercises I have shared with thousands of mamas around the world is linked to this idea of the spiral of life. In fact, I have shared this so often that I now have mamas sharing 'I'm in the middle of a spiral moment!' with their Facebook groups and communities. It's become part of our language. It's something that I am deeply proud of and which has, again, shown me that the Universe is always leading me to what I need to know and share.

I invite you to begin to see all of the challenges you've faced since beginning this experience of matrescence through the lens of the spiral. Here's how …

Take out your journal or laptop, and start by listing all of the dark, hard, challenging moments you've faced since you became a mama. Start from the moment you either started trying to fall pregnant or discovered you were pregnant. If you feel the list is getting too long and overwhelming, just choose the top five.

Then, taking each of your challenging moments, write down what you learnt about yourself through this. Write down where it has led you, or how it has been the beginning of your awakening.

I know that, for some situations, it may still be hard to see the gifts and the growth. In my own journey, it was often not until many years later that I finally saw what a challenging dark time had taught me. If you are struggling to see it, think about what you're doing right now—you're learning and growing by reading this book. Perhaps all those challenges brought you here.

Maybe you're still on the backward spiral. You look at your challenges, and then look at the spiral, and feel like you've been going backwards for a long time now. If so, take a deep breath in and remind yourself that you **trust this process**.

I know this process works for me. I may be in the middle of a 'spiral moment', but boy, when the momentum begins to rise again, it's going to be profound! Trust me, it will be.

CHAPTER 9

FOCUS SIX > CONNECTION

> We think our job as humans is to avoid pain, our job
> as parents is to protect our children from pain, and
> our job as friends is to fix each other's pain. Maybe
> that's why we all feel like failures so often—because
> we all have the wrong job description for love.
>
> — GLENNON DOYLE

Babies turn even the most solid couples into mere acquaintances, simply co-parenting together. Our roles change, our sex lives change, and our deepest desires change—often to sleep. We go from sharing income and dreams to suddenly feeling like we've put our lives on hold for our family, while they (our partners) just keep on going the way they always have. Or so it seems. As advanced as we have become in many areas of women's rights, the fact remains that a man's career is rarely interrupted by children, like a woman's is.

As journalist and author (and mama of three), Annabel Crabb, asks in her book *The Wife Drought: Why Women Need Wives, and Men Need Lives*: 'Why do we assume that women will change the way they work after they have kids, but that men will just keep on working in exactly the same way?'

We either put work outside of the home on hold, or struggle through years of guilt at not being fully present at work and not being fully there for our kids. And even if we are happy to be home raising the kids, there's the judgement that comes from that. How many mothers have felt they have to justify to me why they are staying home with their children, rather than returning to work? They take for granted that I am making some sort of assumption about them because they are 'just a mum'.

Too often, I see mamas feeling guilty because they don't love being home full-time with their children. They tell me, 'I'm so lucky to not have to work', as if the fact that they don't need the income is the only issue here. It's not. Happiness is.

Sara, a former advertising executive who was 'fortunate' enough not to have to return to work after her two daughters were born, felt so much shame around not loving being a stay-at-home mum. She would get on our coaching calls, desperate to understand why she felt the way she did. 'I should be so grateful … so many women don't have the choice to be able to stay at home.' But was this the choice she really wanted? Her marriage was suffering and they were on the brink of divorce, but she couldn't see that maybe her massive shift in identity, income and purpose was affecting more than just the way she felt about another day of KinderGym and playdough.

Yes, some of us are privileged enough to stay home. Some of us are not. But in my many years of listening to the deepest desires of mamas, I know that whether they work or not is actually not the point—it's whether they feel seen and valued in what they do. Again, it's about their identity. It's about redefining who they are, and making sure their partners recognise that too.

Instead, what tends to happen is that women's lives are turned upside down. Then partner returns home, back from 'normal' life, to find us knee-deep in domesticity. *What did you do today?* How I used to hate that question! What do you think I did today, I wanted to scream. Only breastfed every couple of hours; washed everything in sight; went to the shops again; dealt with three meltdowns and two refusing-to-sleep moments; drove around the block seven times so they'd go to sleep. Oh, and wait for it! Watched *Play School* four times!

No wonder there's not much going on in the bedroom. Not that we feel like it anyway. Our bodies have changed in such a way they are often unrecognisable and we worry about 'bits' that might not be appealing anymore. Whoever was the first person to make the suggestion that a man won't want to have sex with you after they have witnessed you giving birth owes married parents everywhere a serious apology. And deserves to pay for couples therapy. It's stuck in our brains. And it's affected how we feel about ourselves, and therefore seriously affected how we connect with our lovers.

Here's the thing though: connecting with our partner is an important part of our lives. It's passionate, it's sensual, and it's really integral to our happiness as women. I'm sure at one stage in your relationship it was a big part of your connection. I don't know about you, but I don't want to go the rest of my life without experiencing passion again.

But how do you get it back, when it's been months between events?

How do you turn it on, when the baby will be awake again in two hours and you **just want to sleep**?

And how do you even feel like it again, when there is that underlying feeling of not being acknowledged for the massive upheaval in your life?

I will be honest and say that during the past decade of parenthood, my marriage often came at the very bottom of the pile. I was so busy splitting my energy between my children, my dreams, and my daily to-do list that my marriage didn't get much of a look-in.

Of course, it's been part of my daily life. Of course, we've squeezed in the date nights whenever possible, tried to keep our sex life going even with more than a decade of broken sleep, attempted to have moments that are about us as a couple and not just as parents.

But in terms of my focus, it's been right at the bottom of the pile. Why? Survival. I thought I was focusing on the bits that needed me most, and I thought I could let my marriage tick along as it was and it would all be okay.

And, in a sense, it was okay. But I don't want okay.

One of my greatest commitments is to never live an unconscious life. I want to check in with myself and what's working—all of the time. Consistently. And if anything is less than a 7/10, then it needs my love and attention.

And so, at the start of 2017 I made a decision. It was New Year's Day, and our whole family was on a beach holiday with our best friends and their kids. I'd turned forty just a few days earlier and feeling the seismic shift a new decade brings. This would be my decade! I'd spent my thirties having babies, and now it was time for me. It felt liberating. Freeing.

When my best girlfriend came home from a beach walk, excitingly telling me she'd booked us both into the local crystal and healing centre for a New Year's psychic reading, I thought, 'Why not?'

Until I walked into the one-hour session and was instantly confronted with a dire future. 'You're marriage is basically over,' this woman told me.

'I'm sorry,' she said, 'I don't usually do this. I usually try to focus on the positive, even if I see challenges in someone's future. But I think you know this too; it's just not going to work. You're going to try your best to "fix it" this year, but it won't work. You're going to get to the point where you give up—and it will be for the best for everyone involved.'

This is what she opened with. All of this within the first five minutes. My head was spinning, my heart pounding, but there was also a feeling of recognition, deep within my belly: yes, it isn't working.

I sat there for nearly an hour in a daze, nodding along and listening, asking questions about how my children would deal with it. How I'd deal with it. How he'd deal with it. The way she described it, we'd all be better off. Even the kids would be happy. And to top it all off, apparently I was going to meet a wonderful new man who I loved and loved us, who made me laugh, and had a beautiful light energy about him. Someone who would lighten up my world. Make me feel adored.

An hour later, I walked out changed. I went back to the holiday house and tried to act normally, smiling at my husband and best friend, giving them vague answers when they asked about the fortune-telling session. But as soon as I could, I found a quiet corner and called my sister. 'Is this true?' I asked. 'Can this really be true?'

Over the coming days, I moved through a number of emotions, mainly anger. How dare this woman do such a thing! How dare she tell me that it was all over, and there was no point trying to fix it. She'd dangled the carrot of a new man in front of me, and everyone being so much better off. And it would have been so easy to accept it.

There is a part of our brain called the reticular activating system, and one of its powerful jobs is to gather evidence of what we believe to be true, filtering out everything else. In other words, once the seeds of divorce had been planted in my mind, that clever little system of nerves in my brain went to work to prove it was correct.

It's so important for us to know this about our brains—and the Law of Attraction. What we focus on expands, in both an energetic way and a physiological way. Our brain and the vibration of our thoughts work to create more of what we're thinking about, whether it's what we want or not. It becomes law.

A week or so after my psychic doomsday reading, I finally broke down and told my husband what had happened. I was so overwhelmed and scared and heartbroken; I couldn't keep it in anymore. His reaction was phenomenal. He didn't laugh or dismiss it as psychic mumbo jumbo, as I had feared. He listened, and heard what I was afraid of. And we decided together that what I'd been told was a prediction of what was going to happen if we didn't change our ways. If we continued on the path we were on, we now knew where we would end up. And we vowed we didn't want that.

So did it all work out beautifully? Actually, no. In fact, it got worse before it got better. But it did get better.

To get to that place, I had to undo some antiquated ideas about relationships, my role and his role, and what I thought I 'deserved'. I had to reunite with him in a whole new way. We had to come back together, new.

So how did we do this? We came back to a core understanding of who I was as a woman, and who he was as a man. We dropped all the old stories and Inner Mean Mama thoughts that were on high rotation (especially since that reticulated part of my brain had now been trained to find all the problems in our marriage). We were honest about the resentment and the anger and the fear and the changes we had felt, but hadn't talked about. And then I completely surrendered the future to the Universe, and decided to focus on what I **did** want. Which was **to feel adored.**

One day when my youngest baby was about two years old, I went along to hear one of my favourite teachers and authors speak: Marianne Williamson. I thought I was there to hear her talk about *A Course in Miracles* (her main teaching topic) and living a more divinely connected life. I thought it would be like one of the many interviews I'd seen her do on *SuperSoul Sunday* and other shows, and so I settled in with my pen and paper to take notes, like the good student I am. Truth be told—I hadn't even looked at the program. I'd seen her name and just signed up, then and there.

Little did I know that the workshop was all about relationships. Right at a time when I hadn't spent a moment thinking about mine! Talk about divine timing.

Over the next few hours, Marianne talked about masculine energy and feminine energy, in a way I'd never heard before. She spoke about the broken-ness of relationships around the world, because of our attachment to masculine ways of thinking and acting. She even called couples up onto the stage to 'counsel' them, then and there, back to love and connection.

Then she shared something that made me sob, right in the middle of the auditorium, among hundreds of others: 'All that is needed in relationships is quite simple: Men need to feel respected, and women need to feel adored.'

The tears flowed—not for me, but for him. For the man I had been pushing away, and not respecting, for years.

She went on to say that men are so much more sensitive than women. They may not say anything, but inside they are crushed. We have a generation of men who feel they are failing because, at their very core, they must feel that they are respected. They must feel like they are a provider, that they are trusted, that they can go out and do what they need to do and return triumphant.

But women are so strong these days, we've taken all that away from them. 'I don't need no man!' we cry. But then we get angry and resentful that our men aren't what we want them to be. We take their belief in themselves away every time we don't let them do something, or we nag them, or we tell them they're not doing it right.

And when we do that, we don't allow them to adore us. Let me say that again: **we don't allow them to adore us.**

They want to protect us. They are built to go out and fight for us, especially once they become fathers. Then this masculine trait is triggered even more. And they want to come home to our soft, nurturing, feminine home and body and feel respected.

Can you understand that? By taking the opportunity to be strong and to provide away from our partner, we are taking their inherent sense of self away; and then they can't adore us in the way we crave.

I sobbed. I cried so much I had to hold my breath to try and contain it.

I do that. I don't respect him. I think I need to do it all, and I just take over. I don't let him do what he needs to do. Life-changing.

Over the next few hours, Marianne went on and on about how our understanding of strength and love has been broken. She shared how women can start to switch off their masculine energy (much of which I have shared with you), and how we can start to honour our men more. She explained that this isn't about surrendering ourselves completely and reverting back to being a 1950s housewife—absolutely not. It's about understanding that in some parts of our lives, we need to be switched on and be all 'masculine action and power'. However, in other parts we do not—especially in our relationship.

I could clearly see that this is exactly what I had been missing.

On the way home that night, I thought about what I should do with all of this information. How could I start to undo a lifetime of believing that my independence, my multi-tasking I'll-do-it-myself energy, was my strength? How could I switch it off a little and allow my husband to step up?

When I got home and the kids were finally in bed, I told him I wanted to talk to him about something, and the look in his eyes broke my heart. He looked scared—not because he thought I was going to break up with him, but because he thought he was going to be told off again. His eyes showed me that he believed I was about to launch into a story of what he was doing wrong, and how we needed to change. I was going to take over again, and take all his feelings of respect away.

This was the biggest realisation of my marriage: **this man doesn't think I respect him.**

We sat down at our kitchen table, and I apologised. I told him what I had learnt that day. I explained why it was the way it was, and how hard it was for me to let go of my control over everything. I said sorry for not respecting him.

He cried. His eyes instantly filled with tears, and his whole body softened. The fear in his eyes at the start shifted to disbelief, and he reached his hand out for me.

There was no judgement from him. I went through everything Marianne had said about women and our struggles over surrendering. He nodded and understood why it was the way it was. But the relief on his face! I will never, ever forget that.

I truly believe that our attempts to be all and do all as women have emasculated our men. I could see it in my own man's eyes that day, and have since seen it over and over again in other relationships around me. We're so in fear of trying to be the best mother and woman and partner and human being, we're pushing away what we most need—to be heard, seen and adored. To surrender to being loved. To feel vulnerable and soft. To feel protected for just a moment.

It's not our fault. Remember, this comes from many lifetimes of programming and survival. But surely it's time to change?

I know it's hard for you to soften, mama. I know you're in the middle of survival mode, and just keeping your head above water. But what if you could soften and ask for what you need? What if you tuned into that Inner Mean Mama voice inside that says, 'He never helps me; why is he so useless? Why do I have to do everything?' and instead explain what you really need, from a place of deep desire to be heard. Not to tell him off, but to speak honestly about how are feeling and what you really need from him.

To soften, we need to switch off our masculine energy. We literally have to turn our feminine energy 'on'. We have to connect with ourselves somehow, before we can connect with our partner—whether it's in the bedroom or just on the couch. When I heard Marianne Williamson speak about this to a captivated room of women, she explained that it takes at least half an hour for us to switch out of our masculine mode of doing, doing, doing, and into our feminine mode of being ready to receive. Half an hour. That means half an hour of actively switching your feminine energy on. What does that look like? Having a bath, lighting a candle, getting out your essential oils, listening to music. **Not** doing the dishes and sorting out the day care bag for the next day.

A relationship is a dance of masculine and feminine energy. If both partners are in their masculine space, then it ain't happening. Nothing you can do about it—it's just not there. It's too yang. It doesn't match, and there's no sparks (well, not the good ones anyway.) And that's what we're doing, mamas—we're living in our masculine. We're all about proving we've got this, so switching over to the feminine feels scary and vulnerable and, perhaps, even weak.

One mama I coached once said to me, 'I'm just all cuddled out.' I thought that was such a great explanation of how it can feel at the end of the day. When you've been so physically attached to your children all day—feeding them, cuddling them, picking them up, carrying them—a hand suggestively reaching out for yours at night can feel too much. We think it's something else we need to 'do'. But it's not. When you truly begin to understand the power of the divine feminine, you will see that this is about receiving. Let yourself be touched and adored. Let yourself receive. Let him show you how beautiful you are, so you can soften into it again.

Parenthood will pass. These crazy-ass days of endless focus on our little ones are just a small part of our entire lives and, hopefully, our entire relationships. But we need this as women—it's a core part of who we are. To be whole and full and able to give, we need to receive. We need to feel adored. We need to see our partner with new eyes. We need to soften and open.

And we need to speak the truth about what we're really scared of and struggling with, without judgement or attack. Chances are, he's just waiting for you to tell him what you need. He wants to give to you and support you—that's his greatest role. He wants to be your protector. He just can't read your mind.

It's been a few years since that fortune teller's dire predictions, and my relationship is better now than it has ever been. I have finally softened into my part of the marriage, receiving him and holding space for him as the divine feminine does. Of course, I still step into my masculine on a daily basis, to run my business and organise the family. But between us, I receive. I see him and all he is doing for us.

I've also spent a lot of time talking to him about matrescence, and the struggles I have felt in finding myself again. How difficult it was for me to walk away from that lifelong career in the media, to be at home with my little blog. I lost myself. I completely lost who I was. And in my attempt to find my way back, I was very angry at him and how 'perfect' his life seemed to be. While I stepped back to do school pick-ups, day in and day out, his career hit new heights. That hurt. But it wasn't until I talked to him about it—without attack or blame, but with true compassion for myself and him—that we finally started to understand each other again.

Now, my night-time ritual for honouring my feminine energy is non-negotiable for our marriage. Every night after the kids are asleep, I take some time to 'switch on'. I dim the lights in the kitchen; I choose an essential oil that feels soft and feminine and sensual for the diffuser; I put my phone away; I pay attention to my body. And even if my Inner Mean Mama voice is still struggling within me at the end of the day, I remind myself how important this relationship is to my own happiness, and I reach my hand out to hold his as we fall asleep.

› Realise that your relationship is new too

Jancee Dunn is mama, wife and author of five bestselling books, including *How Not to Hate Your Husband After Kids*. After her daughter was born, she found herself reverting back to a relationship that resembled the 1950s rather than now, and was filled with anger and resentment. She decided to look into why our relationships change so dramatically, even if they start out with the belief that both parents will play an equal role in child rearing. Many marriage counsellors and interviews with other couples later, Jancee discovered that the biggest struggle within a relationship came from the unspoken changes that occur after the baby comes along.

'There's been a lot of research into how millennials in particular feel about their roles as they enter parenthood, especially men in their twenties. Research shows us that millennials are really determined to divvy up everything 50/50, including childcare and household work. They're all very gung-ho about it. And then, this famous study from Ohio State University followed up with the same couples nine months after the baby was born, and the women had picked up 37 hours extra work a week (both at home and in the workplace if they'd returned). That's more than an extra day's work a week! As one of the authors of the study said: "The egalitarian relationship they had before the baby was born is essentially gone."

'The truth is, in that moment you not only have your world turned upside down, but you also have a stranger who enters your relationship, and demands all of your attention. Before we had the baby, we had all those lovely conversations you have with your partner, like what colour are we going to paint her room, and what are we going to name her. But we really didn't have any of the practical, nitty-gritty conversations at all, like who was going to stay home when the baby was sick, what are our weekends going to be like, and what do you think about timeouts. We just had the fun, superficial stuff. So then, when the baby arrived, there was no time to have a conversation about any of it, or even get our thoughts into some kind of coherent order!'

We seem to be getting better at talking about some parts of motherhood, opening up and being more honest. But when it comes to what happens to our relationship and our sex life, we still seem to hide it from the world. Yet our judgement of how things have changed only adds to the tension.

'There is so much shame around it,' agrees Jancee. 'I remember looking at images of these families with a smiling, gurgling happy baby and the parents looked well-slept and groomed and didn't have stains on them and it was all #soblessed, and feeling so much shame. I felt I couldn't talk to anyone about it. I couldn't talk about it to my mother, because she has a long memory and she'll remember for forty years what Tom, my husband, did. And I felt I couldn't talk about it to my sisters or friends. It's funny, you can talk about your boyfriend's bedroom habits; but when it's your husband you become protective somehow. You don't want anyone to think badly about them.

'But the truth was, we were squabbling all the time and I thought no-one else was. Which, of course, wasn't true. In fact when my book came out, one friend told me that she didn't talk to her husband for two years after the twins were born. And she never said a word to me! This was someone whose father had died and I nursed her through that—emotionally—but she didn't feel like she could talk to me about this.'

So what is the solution? To redefine what each of you need?

'What we need to do is find a balance that feels equitable, and that's going to be different for everyone,' says Jancee. For some, it will mean he makes dinner half of the week; for others, it will be school pick-up days. What I do is take my emotional temperature a lot during the day. I ask myself whether I am feeling resentful. What am I feeling? My husband cooks once or twice a week (let's face it, it's once) and is that equal? It isn't! But it works for me. I like to cook, and once a week off feels like a treat, so I'm okay with that.'

After all the counselling and interviews and insights, Jancee came to two clear conclusions: realise that everyone just wants to be heard; and when you have a baby you have a brand new relationship, so you have to start from scratch.

This is your chance to redefine your relationship, and what it means to be parents **and** lovers. Don't let unspoken antiquated ways of doing things creep in, and don't let your resentment fester. Open up, and talk about what you're feeling. You might find that he is going through his own transformation too.

> Our female friendships

It's not just our men we so long to reconnect with. We miss our sisterhood too. Raising our babies with other women, standing with our tribe, is what is meant to happen. We were never meant to have babies on our own, spending the majority of the day talking to no-one but our toddlers.

Friendships can be tough to maintain with kids. Unless you're having babies at exactly the same time as your girlfriends, different ages can mean very different activities and focus. Not that children of similar ages are always the recipe for strong bonds—mothers groups are either a huge hit or miss for so many mamas. I lucked out with mine. I had a beautiful group of women who held the space for me for many years as a first-time mama. With the birth of my third baby on my own in Sydney,

I missed that regular contact so much I created my own little mothers group with women who are still my closest friends. I know I was lucky.

But it's hard work keeping our friendships alive post-babies. Before bubs, friendships are key to our happiness and a big part of our lives. Girlfriends are meant to be forever, right? If Carrie and her gals from *Sex and the City* managed it, so can we! Babies weren't meant to get in the way of our bonds—just like they were never going to get in the way of our sex life.

Suddenly, our friendships have to fit in around everything else. Text messages before bed, rushed phone calls on the way to work, quick catch-ups after months of rescheduling—welcome to the friendships of motherhood! Career, responsibilities, romance, marriage and now babies all mean our former number one priority slowly slips down our list of frequently dialled numbers. And while some rare female friendships easily readjust to this change in status, many don't. Which can be heartbreaking, right at the time when we so desperately need to feel a connection with another woman.

While researching for a magazine article about female friendship during our thirties, I spoke with Natalie Kon-Yu, co-author of *Just Between Us: Australian Writers Tell the Truth about Female Friendship*. She was pretty clear that the expectations we have on our female friendships—thanks partly to the media—can be harmful.

'*Sex and The City* was such a rare space in our cultural land-scape,' she told me. 'It allowed us to hear women talking to each other about the realities of life; but the idea that four such different women can continue to get along, despite the fact that their lives change immeasurably, is completely unrealistic. It's a myth, and I think it's actually damaging to women, because you tend to blame yourself if you can't hold onto your friendships like that. I remember when my best friend and I fell apart,' admits Kon-Yu. 'I felt so ashamed of myself for not being able to maintain that friendship in the way I thought I should.'

As our new identity emerges, friendships dissolve. Sometimes, part of that shedding of who we used to be ends up including those we were closest to. It's a hard reality, but it's often no-one's fault. In fact, research has found that we end up replacing about half of our friends every seven years. So chances are that if you'd picked six bridesmaids when you were married seven years ago, only three of them would still be your friends now.

Nothing is permanent. Not our lives, nor our relationships. The fact that I didn't have my best friend from my teens and twenties at my baby shower, as I was convinced she would be, was very painful at the time. We grew up together, fell in love with our future husbands together, dreamt of our children growing up together. But right before my engagement, it all fell apart. Looking back, I don't even know why. Sure, there was a nasty argument one night after one too many sauvignon blancs (we were in our twenties after all). But in reality, that's not why it dissolved. What I can see now is that we were beginning to enter that next season of our life, and we weren't aligned in how we were going to do it.

This is the powerful gift of becoming who you really are, and redefining yourself through all of this: we are **becoming**. You have a destiny, a purpose, a path to follow. How can we assume that the person we chose from the small select group of high school friends in our hormone-run teenage years is the perfect companion for matrescence and beyond? We can't.

Some of us choose wisely, and we grow together. But many of us do not. Could not. And that's okay.

The breakdown of that friendship crushed me more than any man ever has. It was the greatest heartbreak of my life. But I know, deep in my soul, that it was not meant to be. We had different ideas and different paths, and I am actually grateful that it disintegrated when it did. It allowed me to step into motherhood completely raw from the heartbreak, but ready to become. Ready to find out who I was now.

Matrescence is a transformation in all areas of your life, including your friendships and your relationship. You are changing, and so too will your connection with the people around you. You want it too. As you rise and evolve and emerge, you will want people who match where you are at that moment in your life. And the more you accept the fact that all facets of you are transforming, the easier the ride will be—and the quicker those new connections will manifest.

If you've lost your tribe, or had your heart broken like only a girlfriend can do, please know that what you are feeling is real. It is important. Grieve for it, like you would an intimate relationship. Again, grieving and acknowledging the transformations is important—without that, we become numb.

When we allow ourselves to grieve the changes within us, and how they are manifesting around us, we then allow ourselves to move through the stages of sadness into hopefulness and then joy. Because I promise you that joy is coming.

You will find your tribe again. You will find a place of women who see you as you really are: magnificent and brave and committed to this transformation. You will shed the old you and the old connections in a beautiful, graceful way, and emerge surrounded by your warrior sisters.

Just start with you. Start by treating yourself as your best friend, and taking yourself out for a date. Get a notebook and write down what you are letting go and what you are welcoming in. The create space for it all to come in.

And remember, this is but a phase. Right now, you're in the chrysalis phase. You're finding your wings. This can be a very internal time in your life, a time of reflection and introspection. Honour that. Your tribe will be waiting for you when you're ready to emerge.

CONNECTION ACTIVITY > Sharing
Your Transformation

Being vulnerable is hard. It's perhaps one of the scariest things we can do. But if we crave connection—which as human beings we do—sharing our true selves with those we love is our only way through, mama.

It's also how we soften and open up to receive. Your feminine energy needs this. It needs you to lower the drawbridge, stop trying to figure it all out on your own, and be ready to receive. Receive a little support, a hug. Your feminine energy craves for you to be seen for what you're really going through, and who you are becoming.

As Brené Brown says: 'He or she who is willing to be the most uncomfortable is not only the bravest but rises the fastest.'

I know these conversations are uncomfortable, but they are imperative for your rising, mama.

Talk to your partner about matrescence, and how you feel you have changed since your first pregnancy. Ask him or her to just listen to you, holding the space for you. Make it clear that this is about you and your struggles, and is not a reflection of what your partner has done right or wrong. Ask to be heard, and share from your heart.

And then in return, ask them how their transformation has been. Do they feel they have really stepped into more like a 'protector' energy? Do they struggle with grieving their past life? What do they long for again?

Sit with each other, and bravely share how you're feeling.

If you don't feel you can do this with your partner, find someone to share this with. A girlfriend, a sister, your mum, or a counsellor. Your transformation needs a witness. It needs to be heard and seen.

It will be confronting. Realising just how much I had pushed my husband away, judged him for his happiness and success, and resented the role I was now playing was deeply unsettling. It brought up a lot of judgement and fear around showing who I really was. But it transformed my marriage. And it continues to transform all of the relationships in my life.

Find someone close to you who you can share this with, and reach out. Your deep desire to be held through this process demands this.

CHAPTER 10

THE BIRTH OF YOU

If nothing more, we have a responsibility to end
the forced choice of a love-it or hate-it narrative
that splits mothers rather than aids them in making
meaning of their motherhood.

— DR AURÉLIE ATHAN

If only we'd known. If only we'd known.

If only we'd had someone tell us that when we first held that baby in our arms, or felt that first kick in our belly, what was about to happen to us was so much more than a new child. It was a new life.

A life that at times would feel like the greatest contradiction: the best and worst; the ending of so much and the beginning of so much.

If only someone had come to my room in the middle of the night, as I paced the floor with my new baby, terrified and alone.

If only someone had told me that when I felt I had to choose my family over my career, I would find something new. Something so much more meaningful and aligned.

And if only someone had shown me that through all of this—the tears, the tantrums, the fears, the brokenness—I would emerge more whole than I ever thought possible.

But it's not too late. It's never too late. In fact, you're exactly where you need to be. You now have a name for what you are feeling. And with a name, the transformation begins.

Over the past decade and more of motherhood, I have screamed at my kids in moments of complete self-pity—too many times to admit. I have slammed doors on their little faces, when it was time for bed and all I could think about was getting into bed myself. I have said 'no' to stories, to treats, to movies, and to more play time, because I was wrapped up in my own woes and couldn't pull back. And I have cried and cried, hiding in the bathroom, begging for things to be different.

As they say in the classics: it didn't happen overnight, but it did happen. It started with questions that I couldn't find the answers for, and desperation to start feeling happy again. It started with the belief that I didn't have to put myself on hold while raising my babies, which then became the realisation that I didn't want to be that woman anymore anyway. It started on that hospital bed when 28 weeks pregnant, with my very first chakra meditation and a complete surrender to the journey.

Yogi Bhajan, the founder of Kundalini yoga, teaches that the very first principle of happiness is commitment. We have to commit to our happiness, to make it an active part of our lives. This isn't a passive thing that just happens. It's about waking up each day and making the choice to do it differently. To find a better way. To reconnect and rediscover who it is you are.

Matrescence requires a commitment, mama. It asks you to acknowledge yourself right now, then hold the space for a more divine version of yourself to be born.

I can promise you that waiting for the baby to sleep, or school to start, or your husband to initiate sex again are not the answers you are looking for. The answer is a promise to yourself that you are going to show up every single day in this journey and be present. You are going to **see** your children and how they are growing. You are going to honour your body and how it has changed. You are going to slow your mind, stop the judgement, and start to connect to something again. You are going to find a way.

It may not happen every day. In fact, let's be honest here and say it won't. But that's not the point! Matrescence is a complete unfolding of the wise mama and woman you are—at times that unfolding will be gentle, at other times brutal. But what I know for sure is that the more we resist acknowledging how much we're changing, the harder it becomes.

So don't deny what is happening within you anymore. You are worth more than that. Show up. Make a commitment. Forgive yourself when those old patterns rear their ugly heads again, and smile. You're a newborn. You're just learning.

Over the years, I have learnt just as much from the brave mamas who share their stories with me, whether online or over Skype, as I have from the thought leaders I have studied and interviewed. Women who have opened up to me—practically a stranger—and shared their innermost thoughts and struggles. Mamas who've been ashamed that they've hit their kids out of frustration, and mamas who still beat themselves up for how little they bonded with their newborn babies.

But over the time we spend together, something starts to change. A spark of realisation is lit that it all begins with them— the love, the forgiveness, the happiness, the mindfulness. It starts with a beautiful dawning of the new you, and the realisation that all you are craving in your life is right there, waiting for you.

This is what Vicki was reaching out for. She is a beautiful mama who first emailed me from the bath one night, in desperation after another terrible day with her two boys. Vicki decided in that moment to do something about it. Over the next few years, she did every program and read everything I provided. She committed to the transformation. She knew she needed to do the work.

About a year after that first desperate email, this is what she sent me:

'Nobody ever listened to me—I wasn't listening to myself.

I struggled to make lasting connections with people—I was disconnected from myself.

I didn't feel appreciated—I put myself at the bottom of my list.

I felt alone and unsupported—I was my own worst critic.'

Vicki is now community manager in my business. I have witnessed her find herself over and over again. She walks through the steps outlined in this book every day. She is a reminder to me that matrescence really is the making of us. It's our chance to create a lasting connection with the most important relationship of all: with ourselves.

I like who I am now—something I could never say before. I know that the connection I now have with my children, my husband, my friends and my family is purely because of the realisations I have had since Scarlett first looked at me with those pleading eyes. The anger that used to burst out of me like venomous spit at them (and myself) is no longer. It's gone. The anger, the resentment, the bitterness, the panic. Gone. Even when I raise my voice because the situation requires it, it is measured. It is a conscious choice.

But most importantly, truly importantly, I know that the connection I have with myself is more than I ever thought possible.

I trust myself, and the Universe. I know that all things happen for me, not to me. I have healed the wounds of my mother's family, that were built on being a martyr and resentment; and I have healed the belief that you have to work hard to gain anything in this life, which came from my father's side of the family. As Kundalini teaches, I have healed seven generations behind me and seven generations before me. And it's all because of motherhood.

This is a gift. If only we were given the space and knowledge to see it.

Our relationship with ourselves must come first, if we are to be happy. The undervaluing of who we are and what we are doing has to end. Our children are watching—and we don't want them to learn that the only way to love someone is to sacrifice yourself and your wellbeing. We don't want them to see that stress is the norm, and that disconnection from our truth is our definition of success.

This is our greatest challenge. One day, we will look back at this time of trying to figure out how to stay sane while juggling it all, and marvel at what we did. But I don't want to look back and wish I'd done it differently. I don't want to miss this time, and screw up my health again. I want to create a new definition of success for my daughters and son—one that shows a woman can be both creative and driven, soft and hard, passionate and compassionate.

That's what our generation of mothers is all about: rewriting the definition of being a woman.

And that's what matrescence is really about. A rising of you, the mother. Welcome to the new way.

It is time to get started. It is time to wake up. Don't wait another minute.

Claim your heart, and claim your glory. You have all you need. Bless other women. Do not tear them down. Remember they are you—your sisters, teachers, mothers, daughters.

And then look on men with the eyes the Goddess gives you, and hold on.

The new world will seem like nothing you have seen before. It will be reborn like you.

It will shine like you. It will smile like you. It will feel like home.

MARIANNE WILLIAMSON

ACKNOWLEDGEMENTS

This book would not be possible without the unwavering and generous support, guidance and wisdom of Dr Aurelie Athan. Never before in my life have I had someone SEE the potential in my ideas, and what I could do in this world. Your willingness to support me, to listen to me and my 'cracking open' moments, and gently guide me to lean in even more, has given me the confidence to step into this work. Thank you for holding the space for me to rise.

There are a number of other women and teachers who have inspired, guided and supported me along the way, without whom I would not be able to share this with the world. Some have been my personal mentors, others have only guided me in their words and wisdom.

Marianne Williamson—although unlikely to read this, I could not do this work without your trainings and inspiration. Your Aphrodite Training changed the course of my life, and my marriage.

Gabrielle Bernstein—I still remember the first time I interviewed you. You were in your pyjamas early in the morning, and your husband brought you a warm drink as we spoke. Your teachings have not only guided me to my own understandings, but your example of how to be a Spirit Junkie and teacher in this world, including showing up just as you are, pyjamas and all, has shaped who I am now.

Marci Shimoff, Debra Poneman and the team of Your Year of Miracles—you came into my life when I needed a miracle. Marci and Debra, you both immediately saw in me what I couldn't see—that this was all possible, and I was ready. Thank you for acknowledging that, and creating opportunities for me. Meta and Suzanne, thank you for allowing me to question it all and then hold the space while I found my way back.

Bronnie Ware—so many interviews, so many times you've said yes to my requests, so many times you've given me goosebumps as we've spoken. Your reminder to allow the space stays with me today. Thank you for your example of a different way.

Rebecca Campbell—for reassuring me of the process, and reminding me I am supported.

Kelly Diels—a late entry! But without you, I know this book and this work would not be reaching as many mamas around the world as it will. Thank you for your fierce commitment to changing the way we honour women, and showing me how to own this superpower.

To my support crew, both in my business and in my circle of influence—Lisa Corduff, who would I be without you?; Vicki Hill, for always having my greatest interest at heart; Mel Donnelly, for stepping in when I was drowning; Stacey Packer, for pushing me to see myself differently; Penny Chalmers, for your support right from the beginning; Debbie Spellman, for our divine Voxer conversations; Nicole Rowan, for helping me see things so differently; Claire Obeid, for your deep friendship; Rosie Barry, for being just as excited about the discovery of matrescence as I was, and backing me all the way.

To my family, thank you. Marque, no matter what, you always say 'Go for it, baby'. I am truly blessed to have such a phenomenal cheerleader. Thank you for creating the most divine cover art for me—I am so proud of all we are creating in this world. Scarlett, Greta, Cassius—my greatest teachers. Being your mama has MADE me. It is an honour to witness your souls evolve in this lifetime. Johanna—for all those crazy kid's dinners, wines, phone calls, and last-minute catch ups, you balance me. You bring me out of my head, and back down to the ground. Thank you. And to my Mum and Dad—always there, always cheering me on, always just a phone call away. Thank you.

Thank you to Elena Brower, Kate Northrup, Sarah Napthali, Dr Catherine Birndorf, Brooke McAlary and Jancee Dunn—your examples of how to do this mamahood thing with grace has not only inspired me on such a deep level, but will now inspire so many others. Thank you for saying yes, and sharing your wisdom with us all.

And finally, to all the mamas—as of writing this, 4500 of you who've signed up to my online programs. My deepest gratitude. Your honesty and vulnerability push me to do this work. Reading your words, hearing your voices on all our live calls, holding space for you is the greatest honour. I promise you—I will not stop here. It's time we honoured motherhood differently, and thanks to your honesty and openness with me, I will continue to go out there and spread the word.

There is a different way.

ABOUT THE AUTHOR

Amy started her 'traditional' career as a journalist at the ABC in 2001, working her way up from producer and news reader in regional South Australia to senior producer at ABC Sydney. During those 15 years, she covered everything from the terrorist attacks of 9/11 to federal elections and natural disasters, and interviewed world leaders and best-selling authors and celebrities. She thought her dream of becoming the Tokyo Correspondent was in her sights.

And then, along came babies.

For the first few years, she found herself simply pushing harder to chase those old beliefs of success. Juggling two children, a full-time role producing Sydney's leading breakfast program (and a 3.30am wake-up call) while starting a blog about her own journey of mamahood, Amy's attempts at 'having it all' came crumbling down when, at 28 weeks pregnant with her 'surprise' third child, she found herself in early labour and at risk of bringing a very small and premature baby into this world. Her addiction to busy-ness had finally caught up with her.

Over the next ten weeks, Amy spent day in and day out lying on the couch, reading everything she could on meditation, mindfulness and energy healing. She studied chakras, got herself a life coach, and committed to changing the old beliefs that had put her unborn baby at risk. Realising that it was her inability to slow down and just be 'okay' with a different pace, she has since been on a mission to unlearn all that she believed about success.

Since the birth of her healthy baby boy at 38 weeks, Amy has slowly stepped back from her ABC career, and in 2015 made the decision to focus 100% on building her work with mamas. She has since coached thousands of women, both one-on-one and in group programs, and is now dedicated to changing the conversation about motherhood and womanhood around the world.

You can connect with Amy on:

Instagram @amytaylorkabbaz
Facebook @amytaylorkabbaz
amytaylorkabbaz.com

We hope you enjoyed this Hay House book. If you'd like to receive our online catalog featuring additional information on Hay House books and products, or if you'd like to find out more about the Hay Foundation, please contact:

Hay House, Inc., P.O. Box 5100, Carlsbad, CA 92018-5100
(760) 431-7695 or (800) 654-5126
(760) 431-6948 (fax) or (800) 650-5115 (fax)
www.hayhouse.com® • www.hayfoundation.org

———

Published in Australia by: Hay House Australia Pty. Ltd.,
18/36 Ralph St., Alexandria NSW 2015
Phone: 612-9669-4299 • *Fax:* 612-9669-4144
www.hayhouse.com.au

Published in the United Kingdom by: Hay House UK, Ltd.,
The Sixth Floor, Watson House, 54 Baker Street, London W1U 7BU
Phone: +44 (0)20 3927 7290 • *Fax:* +44 (0)20 3927 7291
www.hayhouse.co.uk

Published in India by: Hay House Publishers India,
Muskaan Complex, Plot No. 3, B-2, Vasant Kunj, New Delhi 110 070
Phone: 91-11-4176-1620 • *Fax:* 91-11-4176-1630
www.hayhouse.co.in

———

Access New Knowledge.
Anytime. Anywhere.

Learn and evolve at your own pace
with the world's leading experts.

www.hayhouseU.com